At the

Heart

OF EVERY GREAT

Father

CLARK COTHERN

AT THE

Heart

OF EVERY GREAT

Father

FINDING THE HEART OF JESUS

MULTNOMAH PUBLISHERS
Sisters, Oregon

AT THE HEART OF EVERY GREAT FATHER
© 1998 by Clark Cothern

Published by Multnomah Publishers, Inc.

Cover design by D^2 DesignWorks
Cover photograph by Tamara Reynolds Photography

Printed in the United States of America

International Standard Book Number: 1-57673-213-4

Unless otherwise indicated, all Scripture references are from
The Holy Bible, New International Version © 1973, 1978,
1984, by International Bible Society. Used by permission of
Zondervan Publishing House. All rights reserved.
Also quoted:
The Living Bible (TLB) © 1971 by Tyndale House Publishers
The Message © 1993 by Eugene H. Peterson

For information contact:
Multnomah Publishers, Inc.•P.O. Box 1720•Sisters, Oregon 97759

Library of Congress Cataloging–in–Publication Data
Cothern, Clark.
    At the heart of every great father/Clark Cothern.
      p.cm.   ISBN 1-57673-213-4 (paper)
    1. Fathers. 2. Father and child. 3. Fatherhood.
    4. Fatherhood—Religious aspects—Christianity. I. Title.
HQ756.C675   1998   97-32501
306.874'2—dc21   CIP

98 99 00 01 02 03 04 — 10 9 8 7 6 5 4 3 2 1

Dedication

She covered her head with the pillow, trying to muffle the *click, click, click* of the keyboard. The bedroom of our little mobile home was strategically located one thin wall away from the laundry room where my computer sat on a door-turned-desk between the washing machine and the dryer. (I'm still oddly overcome with a compulsion to write every time I hear a rinse cycle. I feel strangely agitated for some reason.)

In fact, her ears rested—or tried to rest—only sixteen inches from the noisy keyboard, since the bed's headboard backed up against the very wall where I sat, jotting down the funny thing the kids did that day "before I forgot it."

Around ten-thirty or eleven I'd kiss her and say, "I shouldn't be too long," and she'd reply, "See you in the morning, sweetheart." But she said it with a smile (most of the time). Then, at 1:00 or 2:00 or 3:00 A.M. as I tried to stealth my way under the covers, she'd half open an eye, say "Good story, huh?" and then roll back over and plummet instantly back into the dark depths of sleep.

That routine began about ten years before Larry Libby called and said, "My first reaction to this manuscript is enthusiastic. I'll see if the other folks at Multnomah are as positive about it as I am."

I couldn't possibly count the number of nights she dealt with this sleep-depriving affliction. You'll be happy to know, however, that since we are no longer in the mobile home and since my computer is located within the narrow confines of our upstairs bedroom, I have, with great self-control, altered my schedule, trying very hard not to write past 11:00 P.M. these days. It makes for better sleep and a more harmonious marriage.

Four feet from the foot of our bed, in the bottom right drawer of my much-too-large desk, there sits a weathered file folder, jammed between "Advent" and "Anger," with titles scratched out and new ones written below them. The final title at the bottom of the list says, "At the heart of every great father." Inside the folder, along with handwritten notes, contracts, and rough drafts, are eight nicely typed letters, each on beautiful stationery, all from well-respected publishing companies. They each say, through carefully crafted words, in one way or another, "Sorry. You've been rejected."

These years of experiences, including the computer in the laundry room, have been the mixing bowl. It took a while to gather all the ingredients for this particular project. Now the cake is finished. Ten years is a long time to bake a cake. Or write a book. Or stay married to a writer.

Joy, you continue to amaze me and those who know me, as you successfully navigate the complex and sometimes very bumpy roads upon which you careen through the roles of wife, mother, friend, lover, counselor, peacemaker, mercy show-er, encourager, pastor's wife, advice giver, secretary, listener, prison minister, companion, and more.

At the heart of every great father is the Spirit, producing those character qualities we call "fruit." There is another factor, though, just as vital. I may not be Sherlock Holmes, but I've deduced that a father wouldn't be a father without a woman to be the kids' mother. Beside every great father is a Spirit-filled woman we call "wife."

This book is lovingly dedicated to you, Joy, because you are the word "dedication" with skin on. You are the real hero of this book. (Well, actually, God is the real hero, and you play the best supporting role.) You have worked incredibly hard for this book by enduring my compulsive behavior for over nineteen years. You are the only person on the planet who patiently put up with the endless revisions and who waited for hours after I said, "I'll be there just as soon as I finish this chapter."

You're the one who worked long hours in the college business office so I could have free tuition. *You're* the one who managed those high-rise office buildings so I could get through seminary in two and a half years instead of five (like many of our friends). *You're* the one who left the cushy comfort of the corporate world so I could fulfill my call and you could wipe noses, bottoms, and tears full-time for twelve years now.

And to top it all off, you've carved a comfortable home out of a pastor's salary. Talk about your delayed gratification!

Joy, I'll love you forever. I'll like you for always. As long as I'm living, your husband I'll be.

Contents

Medicine for Bad-Dad Days *11*

1. At the Heart of Every Great Father
    You'll Find Self-Control *15*

2. At the Heart of Every Great Father
    You'll Find Gentleness *29*

3. At the Heart of Every Great Father
    You'll Find Faithfulness *47*

4. At the Heart of Every Great Father
    You'll Find Goodness *65*

5. At the Heart of Every Great Father
    You'll Find Kindness *81*

6. At the Heart of Every Great Father
    You'll Find Patience *95*

7. At the Heart of Every Great Father
    You'll Find Peace *109*

8. At the Heart of Every Great Father
    You'll Find Joy *131*

9. At the Heart of Every Great Father
    You'll Find Love *149*

10. At the Heart of Every Great Father
    You'll Find Jesus Christ *173*

Final Thanks *197*

Medicine for Bad-Dad Days

Walter watched his plane take off without him.

Don't you just hate it when that happens? Leaves you with a sinking feeling in your gut. But most of the time, it's just a matter of inconvenience. You can usually wait a couple hours and catch another plane.

Walter couldn't do that.

Walter was the pilot.

At 2:03 P.M. Walter's spirits soared as he inspected the plane's engine, preparing for a fun little dash into the atmosphere. At 2:04 P.M. his heart sank into his socks.

The pilot's eyes bugged as he watched the plane pull at the tie-downs like a balky stallion, yank 'em loose, and gallop down the runway toward freedom. Walter hurled himself in pursuit, racing after his runaway airplane (and wondering all the while what he was going to do if he *caught* it).

The plane lifted off and flew about seventy-five feet then touched down again. That's when Walter really *did* catch his plane. By the wing strut. Hanging on for dear life, he forced the plane to taxi around in small circles.

Several minutes of Walter's dizzying daredevil feats drew a small crowd of amazed onlookers.

They gaped as the plane knocked Walter to the ground— three times! They watched with wonder as Walter sprang to his feet each time, clutching the plane again and whirling in circles.

Exhausted from his air aerobics, Walter lay on the tarmac,

shaking his head, thinking, *This is insane!* (I would tend to agree with him.) After one last mad sprint for the friendly skies, his plane finally came to rest with the assistance of a nearby utility pole.

Walter was treated and released from a Columbus, Ohio, hospital.

Now here's the kicker. The problem that started this whole mess was something small. (Isn't that usually the case?) A tiny two-dollar part caused the throttle on the engine of the spunky little two-seater plane to stick open...leading to Walter's very bad day.

From one dad to another...ever had one of those days when things were going great one minute and then *BOOM,* something happened and you had a bad-dad attitude attack and ship wrecked the whole day?

I sure have. In fact, if I'm going to come clean and get real honest, I'll have to admit that I've had quite a few of *those* days. I've ended up feeling like Walter, going three rounds with a renegade airplane.

Please tell me you've had days like that, too. You have, haven't you? Days when you felt...

- too wrapped up to wrestle your runaway schedule?
- too frazzled to fight the latest parenting battle?
- too tired to tackle the latest kid problem?

And have you noticed, as I have, that it's usually something small that trips the throttle? Or it's a series of small storms that whip up a whirlwind? And when the storm hits, your spirit sinks suddenly into the pits. Or your anger meter jumps into the red zone.

You probably haven't bounded after any breakaway planes lately, but you have no doubt faced an angry kid who made you feel like dusting his crops...haven't you?

That's what it feels like when you have those terrible bad-dad attitude attacks. Almost all dads can relate.

- I've talked with a busy businessman who swam easily through an over-the-banks budget...yet felt like a fish out of water when his daughter wanted to "express herself" about "this boy" she'd been "seeing."

- I've had coffee with a pressured pastor who rained down fire from heaven on Sunday morning only to have a rebellious son rain on his parade by Sunday evening.

- A hard-working factory man confessed to me that he tried to prove his metal by working twelve hours a day, seven days a week, yet felt like jelly when his kids pressed him for more time at home.

- A dedicated deacon told me he felt like a fatherly flop when his do-right daughter didn't.

- And I've listened as an energetic middle manager told how he implemented innovations and worked miracles at the plant yet muddled a simple mealtime because he couldn't talk with his kids without exploding.

Just because we "do the right things"—earn a family wage, show up at church, read the right books, and even spend "quality time" with our kids—doesn't mean we won't also feel like frazzled, forgetful, fatigued failures at times.

But guess what, guys? There is help.

———⟨∂∕∂⟩———

At last and just in time: Here's a prescription-strength remedy for sad-dad days and bad-dad attitude attacks.

Are you poor on patience? Short on temper? Long on mistakes? In need of a few winning plays from the guy who consistently scores relational touchdowns? If so, I'd like to introduce you to someone who wrote the playbook on perfect parenting. Jesus Christ.

I pray, as one dad to another, that together we'll find growth through clenched teeth and comfort in Christ's care for guys like us.

His Spirit is available to lift your spirit.

Blessed are you sometimes-frazzled dads because yours is the kingdom of heaven.

Faithful fathering is not taught. It's caught. One heartbeat at a time. That's why your Father gave you a good example of someone who did it right. He gave you that role model in the form of His Son, Jesus. That's the action picture I hope will take shape in the pages of this book. Real-life, down-to-earth, role-model fathering in action.

So read on and catch little glimpses of a huge heart. See and hear and touch and taste all the qualities that are deep in the heart of every great father.

Hang on, frazzled dad. Hope is about to make a landing.

CHAPTER ONE

At the Heart of Every Great Father
You'll Find Self-Control

—*രെ*—

I swiped at my left shoulder with the fingers of my right hand. Blood! *Yes*, I said to myself, *this is another fine mess you've gotten us into, Ray!*

Ray Aguilera had asked me if I wanted to play a little "pickup basketball."

I'd shrugged and said, "Sure." With my height advantage, I figured I could give Ray a run for his money shooting a little hoop.

Ray was a foot shorter than I and about ten years older, so I thought when he asked me to join him for a game of "pickup basketball" he meant we would "pick up" a basketball from his house on the way to his driveway.

Not exactly.

He already had a basketball in the trunk of his car. Ray drove me over to the "bad" side of South Phoenix to a city park where the cinder-block bathrooms were decorated with a rainbow assortment of gang graffiti and words my mother would never have allowed me to say—much less write—in public.

I stepped out of Ray's little Datsun and narrowly missed planting my right foot on a half-filled Coors bottle. The aroma of stale beer raced its way up to my nose at the same time the scent of a barbecue grill wafted over from a nearby pavilion. The two odors tied, blending for a wonderful first impression of this quaint hideaway.

A quick survey of my new surroundings revealed one fellow, probably ten years younger than he looked, sleeping (or passed out) on a park bench under the shade of a scraggly paloverde tree, and two muscle-bound athletes over on the cement basketball court. They were swishing from thirty feet out.

It became obvious to me that Ray "I-can-whip-you-even-if-you-*are*-twice-my-size" Aguilera intended for both of us to play both of them.

"Ray," I said, shaking my head, "this is a big mistake."

I saw Ray's mouth moving but didn't hear any words, because just as he spoke, a low rider cruised by, pulsating a stream of rap music, the bass tones bulging the car windows with each *boom-boom-CRASH, boom-boom-CRASH* until it vibrated our fillings.

Ray could tell from my pained expression that I hadn't received his last transmission. He tried again. In his characteristic exaggerated Hispanic voice, Ray razzed, "C'mon, Clarkie boy. It'll do you some good. Don't be afraid. There's a phone a half-mile away. I can always call 911 when you get hurt."

I wasn't laughing. I was sweating.

We walked up to the courts, glass crunching beneath our sneakers. I tried to follow Ray's lead and act tough. Imagine an almost-6'-tall, skinny white boy strutting alongside a 5'2", bald-headed Mexican. We must have looked entertaining. They asked if we wanted to join them.

I really wanted to say, "So kind of you to ask. I can see though that you gentlemen are terribly busy. Sorry to have bothered you. Thanks for your time." Instead, knowing Ray was never going to let me forget it if I backed out, I just stood there with a blank stare, shaking my head yes.

It was obvious from the outset that I was dead meat. Those two moose elbowed all the way to the basket. This was not at all like playing "horse" in the driveway back home. They didn't even let me shoot without trying to block the ball. Boy, was I naive. I was getting stomped. And Ray was getting amused.

I guess he knew I was getting a taste of the real world outside the ivy halls of the college library and away from the ivory palace of the church office over on Central Avenue where I worked.

Our two-man team's only asset was little Ray. The man was quick. Like that little guy in *The Karate Kid*, Ray "waxed on" and "waxed off" all the way down the court.

As we battled our adversaries, Ray and I ribbed each other as only close friends can. I could say nonpolitically correct stuff to Ray back then—jabs that would probably get me twenty years today. He cheerfully gave it back in kind; maybe that's a sign of true friendship.

I teased my little buddy about his bald head. "Hey, Ray!" I'd shout, shielding my eyes. "How about gettin' a baseball cap, man? I can't see the basket for the light. It's blinding me, dude!"

This teasing became my strategy against the two big-city bad boys. I'd crack a joke. The two jocks would laugh. While they were distracted, Ray would execute a perfect pick and roll. He would be up, and the ball would be in before they knew what hit 'em. I would pump my arm and say, "Yes!" And Ray would just smile.

That happened three or four times. I fed Ray. I ran around a lot. I cracked jokes. Ray faked, ducked inside, and scored. What a team. I thought, *Abbot and Costello, eat your hearts out.*

I felt like I'd finally found my niche. I was the comic-relief portion of this basketball program, and we were starting to rack up an impressive lead.

That's when it stopped being so funny.

Our serious opponents didn't think it was too cool that this little bolt of Mexican lightning was actually outscoring them. They started fouling both of us...hard.

Ray just kept playing his best. I, on the other hand, complained. They just laughed and took the ball out. I got edgy. Ray could tell I was getting hot under the holy collar. He said, "Clarkie boy. Lighten up. It's cool."

But it wasn't cool. And I was feeling anything but light. Those goons kept elbowing me in the ribs, practically knocking me off the court. I grabbed the ball once and slammed it into the ground, making it bounce twelve feet into the air. On its return trip it almost made a basket, so I almost laughed. But I reminded myself that I was busy getting angry.

Ray took me aside for a second. He knew something I didn't. He knew our opponents were *trying* to get my goat. He knew that if I got mad enough to fight, they would cheerfully slam-dunk my head.

He waited until our new pals were at the other end of the

court and told me again—a little more forcefully. "Clarkie. Suck it up, dude. Let it roll off, baby. It's just a game. See?"

I was glad he kept me in check, because it made me feel like he was holding me back from killing these two guys...you know, like a poodle being held back from chewing up a couple of pit bulls.

Although my lungs were burning like Arizona blacktop, I kept my emotions cool—for a minute or two. One forceful elbow in my gut though, and I just about blew a gasket. This time Ray knew I was ready to do something stupid. I was working myself up to a real, honest-to-goodness attitude attack. My strategy had been transformed from crack-them-up to crack-them-over-the-head. My ears were almost as red as the blood on my shoulder where they had just scratched me. They said they were "just going for the ball." Uh-huh. With fingernails?

Ray knew I needed a quick shot of "clot buster." He knew the anger boiling in my blood was keeping the oxygen from getting to my brain. He knew I was thinking with my emotions—emotions that were pegging the meter on "MAD."

He took me aside again, looked me straight in the eyes, and said, *Clark!* No more Clarkie boy. He was serious. "Shake it off. *Now!* Two more points, and they win. It's not worth it. There's more at stake here than a game, okay? Now c'mon. Be a man."

Though my brain was foggy, Ray's last three words cut through like a foghorn: "Be a man."

I caught his point. These guys weren't playing basketball; they were playing "King of the Mountain." They were getting what they wanted. They wanted to win at any cost. They wanted to make us look and feel lower than they were. And if I got mad enough, I would make their game even better. I was about to play into their hands. I was about to stoop lower than the lowest. I was about to act stupid.

Thanks to Ray's coaching, I took a deep breath, trotted down the court, and acted like a man. We played the last two points. They won the battle of basketball. I won the battle of anger, with Ray's help.

We shook hands. We went back to Ray's car. After I slumped into the front seat, shut the door, and locked it (quickly), relief began to soak into my aching bones. I was grateful I wasn't lying in an emergency room covered with contusions or shot full of holes.

We got back into the "safe" zone, near the church parking lot where I had left my car. I got out. Ray gave me a high-five. "Good job, Clarkie boy. You did all right...for a skinny guy with chicken legs."

I laughed, "Thanks Ray. Let's do this again sometime. In a couple of years."

I drove home thinking about that high-five from my friend. The high-five at high noon had been a reward for showing some self-control at the showdown.

Fortunately, Ray had displayed more guts than I had, and he taught me a lesson: *To be a man means to act like one, even when you don't feel like it.* Sometimes what it takes to "be a man" is brains enough to realize you're overmatched. Being a man doesn't always mean being able to beat the other guy. Sometimes it means doing the best you can with what you've got...and living to tell the story.

The high-five felt good. It meant Ray was proud of me. I

had handled myself without completely losing my cool. I had taken abuse and had refused to give it back. Kenny Rogers was right. Sometimes you've got to "know when to walk away..."

I was grateful the Lord had sent me a mentor. Ray hadn't taken me out on the court to coach me on basketball. He had driven me to the edge of my emotions to teach me about self-control.

I'm not the only one who gets steamed, though. There's a story found in Matthew 26:47–56 that reveals a guy who was ready to slam-dunk some soldiers when they arrested Jesus.

It seems Jesus had taken some of His closest friends out to the bad side of Gethsemane to teach them a lesson, not about swordsmanship, but about self-control, about being a man.

When it became obvious that the other team intended to win at all costs, "one of Jesus' companions reached for his sword, drew it out and struck the servant of the high priest, cutting off his ear" (Matthew 26:51).

If my friend Ray were playing the part of Jesus in this drama, he would say, "Hey, suck it up, dude. Let it roll off. There's more at stake here than winning, okay? These guys aren't playing the same game you're playing. Just a couple more hours and it'll all be over, so just chill, all right?"

Jesus knew He was far more powerful than these "hoods" who came with swords and clubs to take Him by force. He knew He could have called a whole dream team of angels and clobbered them but good.

But He also knew there was a greater lesson to be learned by all who watched. He knew they would see what it means to use self-control, see how to yank back on the reins and demonstrate a powerful strength of character instead of kicking in the spurs and letting loose a stampede of brute force.

Just as Ray calmed me down, Jesus did the same for His team. He revealed a strength that was found in the heart of His Father, and He lost a battle to win the war.

When our youngest daughter put us to the test, my wife, Joy, and I discovered that the weapon of self-control works just as well today as it did back in that garden with Jesus.

We received some in-the-trench weapon training when we arrived at little Derrek's house after his birthday party.

Everyone was all smiles for the first five minutes. Callie was jumping on the trampoline with the perpetually cute, blond-headed little Derrek as all the other kids were leaving with their moms and dads, waving good-bye, and wiping cake from their mouths.

Prepared for the same happy, hasty exit, Joy said, "Callie-Wallie, it's time to tell Derrek good-bye and thank you."

"I don't *want* to go," she huffed, and sat down on the trampoline, tuning herself up for a melodiously good cry.

Tender little Derrek, Callie's six-year-old buddy and problem solver, crawled over to her, cradled Callie's head in his lap, and rocked back and forth gently.

"It's okay," he whispered. "You can come back again sometime."

Joy and I smiled at Derrek's parents. How sweet.

Seeing that we were all enraptured by Derrek's nurturing

move, Callie attempted to catch us off guard, sneak inside, and take the ball to the net. "Can I spend the night with Derrek tonight?"

Eyebrows went up all around, and Derrek's parents stifled the same chuckles Joy and I were fighting.

"Uh, well, no, Callie. We'll explain that a little later, but right now, honey, we have to go because the party's over and everyone else has gone too."

Cue the tears.

Man, did they ever flow. Callie cried, and cried some more. As the crying turned to wails, Joy and I were faced with a decision. We could either physically pick her up and carry her to the car, or we could stay out there in the backyard held captive by a six-year-old with twelve-gauge tear ducts.

Because of the boot camp lessons from veteran dad soldiers like Ray Aguilera, I remembered there was more at stake than simply "winning the battle." This was a time when I could have easily won the game of King of the Mountain. After all, I was much bigger and stronger than Callie.

But I had to remind myself that there was a much more important battle being fought here. If I stooped to her level and threw a fit myself, what would I teach her? That I was capable of acting like a six-year-old?

Joy calmly said, "Well, it looks like we'll have to be the adults here. Let's carry her to the car."

Flashing a "here goes nothin'" smile, first at each other and then at Derrek's parents, we said, "Excuse us, but we'll have to take matters—and Callie—into our own hands. Sorry to have to leave this way, but she has to learn she can't get her way by throwing a fit."

And with that, Joy grabbed Callie's bottom half, I grabbed her top half, and together we smiled and steer-wrestled our way to the car, with Callie fighting and screaming the entire sixty yards.

We calmly endured the noisy five-minute drive home, and when Callie was successfully herded into her room, she continued to vent her frustration, only to discover that throwing a fit did *not* in fact produce the desired effect.

After she spent some "down time" in her room, Callie then spent some time with her mom, talking about why she felt the way she felt. Joy explained, "Honey, screaming and kicking don't get you what you want. We love you, but we can't let you stay somewhere to play longer just because you throw a fit. There will be other times to play with Derrek."

Oh, I wish I could say I always handle every crisis-parenting situation with such control. But that would be a lie. There have been times when the molten lava of my temper has erupted through my calm crust, cascading into a full-fledged, adult temper tantrum with explosive noise I'm sure exceeded the decibel level of Callie's performance.

But each time I'm tempted to play King of the Mountain, I'm reminded that the strongest dads in the world are the ones who can keep their own anger from kicking out the stalls and stomping around like a wild stallion.

And every time my kids see me step up to the plate, acting like an adult, playing referee to my own anger before I have to get called "out" by an embarrassing display of temper, they see a world-class exhibition of the Holy Spirit—the invisible force of the heavenly Father Himself—at work in my life. That's when they learn a little self-control themselves, by example.

My father gave me a great example of self-control when I was a boy watching a church-league softball game.

Dad was forty-three at the time and very active. Though he wasn't known for hitting grand slams, he was good at placing the ball and beating the throw. Singles and doubles were his specialty, and he did the best he could with what he had.

This particular dusty, hot Phoenix evening, Dad poked a good one right over the second basemen's head, and the center fielder flubbed the snag and let the ball bloop between his legs.

My dad saw this as he rounded first base, so he poured on the steam. He was 5'10", 160 pounds, and very fast. He figured that if he sprinted for third and slid, he could beat the throw.

Everyone was cheering as he sent two of his teammates over home plate. The center fielder finally got his feet under him and his fingers around the ball as Dad headed toward third. The throw came as hard and fast as the outfielder could fire it, and Dad started a long slide on that sunbaked infield. Dust flew everywhere.

The ball slammed into the third baseman's glove but on the other side of Dad—the outfield side—away from a clear view by the ump who was still at home plate. Our team's dugout was on the third base side of the diamond, and every one of the players had a clear view of the play.

Dad's foot slammed into third base a solid second before the ball arrived and before the third baseman tagged his leg. But much to the amazement—and then dismay—and then anger—of the team, the umpire, who hesitated slightly before making his call, yelled, "Yerr *out!*"

Instantly, every member of Dad's team poured onto the field and started shouting at once—a scene probably reminiscent of the Garden of Gethsemane just prior to the ear-slicing event. Dad's teammates were intent on only one purpose: They wanted to win, and by golly they knew they were *right!*

The two runners who had crossed home plate before Dad was called out had brought the score to within one. If Dad was out—and we all knew he wasn't—his team was robbed of a single run.

With only one inning left, this one bad call could cost them the game.

But just as the fracas threatened to boil over into a mini-riot, Dad silenced the crowd. As the dust settled around him, he held up a hand. "Guys, stop!" he yelled. And then more gently, "There's more at stake here than being right. There's something more important here than winning a game. If the ump says I'm out...I'm *out.*"

And with that, he dusted himself off, limped to the bench to get his glove (his leg was bruised from the slide), and walked back into left field all by himself, ready to begin the last inning. One by one, the guys on his team gave up the argument, picked up their own gloves, and walked out to their positions on the field.

I've got to tell you, I was both bewildered and proud that night. My dad's character was showing, and it sparkled. He may have been dusty, but I saw a diamond standing out there under the lights, a diamond more valuable than all the points his team might have scored.

For a few minutes that evening I was a rich kid, basking in my father's decision to be a man, to hold his tongue instead of wagging it, to settle the dust instead of settling a score. I knew his character at that selfless moment was worth more than all the gold-toned plastic trophies you could buy.

I was inspired by a guy who demonstrated the same quality that has also been found on basketball courts, in gardens like Gethsemane, and in backyards after birthday parties.

Dad held court that night. Not a basketball court, like my friend Ray, but a court nevertheless. And the verdict came down as hard as a slam dunk. He was convicted of being a man...and the evidence that proved it was his powerful use of that awe-inspiring weapon.

Self-control.

CHAPTER TWO

At the Heart of Every Great Father
You'll Find Gentleness

———*ᵥⁿᵥ*———

Y ou did *what?!*" I fumed, louder than I had intended.

My son, "little Clark," looked even smaller than his six years. He seemed to shrink in embarrassment as I puffed up with anger.

"I guess I lost my key," he mumbled, looking at the ground.

I looked from his red face to the locked bike and down to his feet, which were shuffling.

At that moment I had at least three options.

A. I could have patted him on the head and said, "That's okay, Son. I've lost things, too. I'll help you look for it when I get home from work."

B. I could have gathered my composure and said, "I'm upset right now, but it's not the end of the world. I'll go to my meeting, and after I get home, we'll talk about this when I'm not so upset, okay?"

C. I could have blown up like a pressure cooker with its lid unscrewed too early and said, "I TOLD you that if you wanted a lock for that bike you would have to take responsibility for the key. I can't walk around keeping track of your stuff for you. I guess you can't ride your bike today. If we can't find the key, I'll have to cut the lock off, and it'll be ruined."

Oh man, I really wish I'd chosen Option A.

And failing that, it would have been so great to say I selected Option B.

But I didn't. In this instance, I jumped directly to Option C. I blew up and, as Howard Hendricks is apt to say, gave him a piece of my mind I couldn't afford to lose.

The Clarkster practically bit a hole in his lip trying not to cry. I stomped off to the car and slammed the door as he walked like a little soldier to his room—where I'm sure he fell apart. I can bet he had a lousy morning at school.

Yeah, he's the Little Clark and I'm the Big Clark. I'm stronger than he is. Bigger. Louder. And I had the advantage. He had messed up, and I was in a position to tell him about it, and boy, did I tell him. I was sure that my speech (which was really just a grown-up temper tantrum) had taught him that proverbial Lesson-He-Would-Not-Soon-Forget.

Little did I know I would be in for a lesson of my own later that afternoon.

I drove ninety minutes to my meeting, and by the time I arrived, I had completely forgotten about the lost-key incident. Instead, I was clearly focused on the order of business for the day.

Six long hours later when I left the building, I was still so focused on business that I grabbed my calendar notebook and made a beeline for the car, the same way I had hurried off a dozen times before.

An hour and a half later, as I approached my driveway, a

sinking feeling began deep down in the pit of my stomach. I retraced my steps that morning and recalled how upset poor Clarkie had been after I had chewed him out.

In my mind I replayed the hurt look on his face as I had settled myself in the car, placing my briefcase on the backseat and...*my briefcase!*

I hardly ever took my briefcase to those meetings...but today I had. And why? Because I had planned to drop by the bank on the way home to deposit...*my paycheck!*

Now I admit, it's pretty dumb to forget your briefcase in a building ninety minutes from where you live. It's even dumber to leave your paycheck in that briefcase, especially with bills to pay that weekend and especially when the building containing your briefcase will be empty all weekend.

All the way into the house I shook my head. I quickly walked to the phone and called the office. As I punched in the numbers on the phone, I felt my heart beating and heard the blood surging through the veins in my temples. My ears were red hot. I was looking at my feet, which were shuffling uncontrollably.

Then it hit me.

I was feeling exactly the way my son must have felt earlier that day. My face changed from eat-crow crimson to shame red. My wife entered the room after I had explained my problem to a secretary and just as I said, "Is anyone going to be there later this evening? No? Uh, does anyone live out this direction? Okay, thanks. I'll hold."

Ah, the wisdom of wives. They have a sixth sense for this kind of thing. She said, "Clarkie told me what happened this morning."

I kept the phone to my ear and just nodded my head up and down. I chewed my bottom lip. She continued, "It seems somebody forgot where he put his key." Again I nodded. Just then the secretary came back on the line, and I held up my finger toward my wife in order to say, "Just a second."

I exclaimed, "He is? Oh that's great! Seven o'clock? Fine. That'll be a lifesaver. Thanks!" I scribbled the name of a restaurant into my calendar. And as I looked up, my wife was looking at me with "that look."

"*What?*" I asked, trying to act innocent.

She said, "I don't know *anyone else* who EVER forgets where HE puts things..." and she paused (mercilessly) for effect, tightening her gaze before adding the coup de grâce, "do you?"

I smiled in spite of myself. I'd been had. I called the kids into the room so I could explain they were going to have to miss their evening of TV and pizza so we could all go on a long drive. They moaned.

Glancing away from my wife's impassive face, I continued, "Um, do you remember this morning when a certain somebody lost his key to the bike lock?" My son recoiled like I was about to grind a handful of salt into his already-sore wound. "Well," I went on, "it seems *someone else* in the family has lost something." I looked from face to face.

"Like," I looked straight at Clarkie, "a briefcase." The lad's eyes grew suddenly wide. "And the briefcase just happens to be in someone else's car right now, because he's taking it to a restaurant where I can get it back." The two girls looked at me with faces that scolded, *Dad, how could you?*

"And," I added, dropping the last shoe, "we can't eat supper until I get the briefcase back because—" This time it was my turn to pause for effect, and all eyes narrowed as they awaited my big news— "I left my paycheck in the briefcase."

Suddenly everything erupted but differently than I had expected. Our two daughters both said, "Da-ad!" and shuffled off to their rooms to get ready for our out-of-town excursion.

But my son surprised me.

He walked over to me and nearly knocked me off balance throwing his arms around me.

"Oh, Dad," he said, "it's okay. We all lose things once in a while."

That Sunday as I stood before our congregation to preach, I noticed my son sitting very attentively on the second pew from the front. I told a story based on Matthew 18:21–35 about a man who was really upset.

It seems he owned a business that manufactured briefcases. People were buying laptop computers that year instead of briefcases, and his business didn't do well at all. In fact, he owed five hundred grand to the bank. There was no way he was going to be able to pay back the half-million dollars. The man pleaded with the bank president. He said, "I'm working on a killer new briefcase design for next year. This one'll sell a million! It holds a laptop, cell phone, and a minifax machine. Please give me another chance!"

Fortunately for him, the bank president was a gentle man and very reasonable. He told the fellow, "You don't have to pay me back. I've been in worse scrapes than you, and I know what it means to be forgiven. Go ahead and build that new design this year. And when you do well, just be sure to give me one for Christmas."

The man was overjoyed. He couldn't believe it! As he practically skipped out of the bank to go celebrate, he bumped into one of his middle managers, who just happened to owe him fifty dollars.

"Hey, buddy," he barked, wiping the delighted smile from his face, "pay up. Things have been tight lately, and I want my fifty bucks!"

The little man pleaded with him, "Please—just give me a little longer. I—I'll come up with the money, I promise. I just don't have it today. I had to buy antibiotics for my three kids."

"Nope. You've had enough time. I'm taking you straight to small claims court."

And just about that time, the bank president was on his way out the door to run down the street to Max O' Millions for a "Frugal Burger" when he overheard his recently forgiven client reaming out the poor guy who only owed fifty dollars.

He walked over and tapped the angry briefcase inventor on the shoulder.

"Let me get this straight," he said. "I just forgave you a loan of five hundred thousand dollars...and *you* are going to take this man to small claims court for a debt of *fifty dollars?*"

"Uhm...but...well," was all the man could stammer.

"That does it," said the bank president. "The loan's back on, and if you can't pay it by this Friday, I'm throwing the book at you. You deserve everything you get if you can't even forgive such a small amount." As he stormed off down the street, he could be heard muttering, "And after what I did for him..."

After church I asked my son, "Did you understand the story?"

Clarkie flashed a tentative smile at me and said, "I think so."

I picked him up and hugged him. "Son," I said, "I'm the one who was forgiven a huge debt. My forgetfulness was much worse than yours. I'm the one who should be the most grateful. Thanks for *your* forgiveness."

His small, sheepish grin ripped wide open into a gigantic smile. He hugged me back.

It felt great to be back on good terms with my boy again.

Where do we dads find true gentleness? One place is smack-dab in the middle of our own mistakes, where we recognize our faults. It's a lot easier to be gentle on our kids when we know we can be just as guilty as they are for the things we get so upset about.

The next time Clarkie forgot something, instead of slamming my mouth into high gear and leaving verbal tire tracks all over his countenance, I shifted into neutral and idled long enough to remember an important lesson on forgetfulness. It seems I had gone to driver's school on the word *gentleness*.

In contrast with my own lack of gentleness over the bike-lock incident, I remember a lesson learned from my father the night my sister nearly killed us while she was learning to drive.

On the way home from church one Sunday night, Kathey hit the brakes and cranked the steering wheel sharply to the left to avoid (are you ready for this?) a tiny field mouse.

The old Chevy wagon's rear end lurched wildly around into a slide. Kathey quickly overcorrected, and the car's rear wheels slid back around in the other direction, coming dangerously close to the steep banks of an eight-foot-deep irrigation ditch just off the shoulder.

I was sandwiched in the backseat between my mother on one side and an elderly lady, Mrs. Kench, on the other. With each sudden change in direction, the ladies involuntarily switched their directions of leaning, squishing me first one way and then another. I felt like the creamy center to a very squeezed sandwich cookie.

My father, seated (or at least *trying* to be seated) in the passenger side of the front seat, finally grabbed the steering wheel, holding it steady long enough for the car to jump back into a straight line.

My sister locked up the brakes and skidded quickly to a stop at the side of the highway. Our side-to-side backseat dance was over, and our three heads jolted forward and then back against the seat in concert with the car's arrested motion.

Kathey sat behind the wheel, shaking and sobbing.

"I c-can't drive anym-more. Dad, you—*(sniffle)*—have to drive. I'll *kill* us all."

With my eyes stuck wide open and my fingers welded to my knees, I awaited Dad's next sentence while inwardly shaking my head "Yes!" hoping to invisibly influence my father in the decision to hop behind the wheel.

My father could very easily have yelled at my sister, humiliating her, causing her to sit in miserable silence all the way home as she pondered her lifelong future as a pedestrian.

Instead, in a voice both firm and gentle, he said, "Take a few deep breaths." (We all did in response to his suggestion.) "Now Kathey, you may always fear driving if you don't get back on the road. When you're ready, drive the rest of the way home. I know you can do it."

I prayed for angelic protection and crossed my fingers, but Kathey drove *very* safely all the way home. I've got to hand it to her; she acted with extreme bravery that night by colliding with her fears head-on.

All of us in the car learned from my father that gentleness, blended with firm instruction, makes for a very tasteful and satisfying lesson.

I wish I could have remembered that lesson long enough to apply it the day my son lost the key to his bike lock, but some lessons, like the one about briefcases and forgetfulness, have to be reviewed from time to time, like the multiplication tables. The more you practice, the more they sink in.

One such lesson sank into my young skull while I listened to a schoolteacher reading a story. She was holding a class of normally squirrely children spellbound with a story based on an Eskimo legend. It was about a gentle little girl and a huge, strong, white bear.

As I recall, the burly bear was vacuuming up all the fish in the area, and the village people were afraid they would starve if they couldn't catch any for themselves.

The girl was sent to try to tame the wild bear.

At first the little girl thought she'd been given an impossible task. She felt so tiny and inadequate. She asked herself, *Why me?* But before she could answer herself, she remembered her father's words, the ones he used to say to her whenever she attempted a hard task: He would say, "Why *not* you?"

So, as she made her way to the bear's lair, she thought, *Yes. Why* not *me?*

Soon she located the bear.

She observed that the bear ran quickly across the Arctic ice because of the tufts of fur growing between its toes on its big paws. She waited until the bear dozed off after a huge fish dinner. As the bear lay sleeping, the gentle little girl crept up to it and quietly snipped the fur from between the toes on all four paws.

Just as the bear awakened, the little girl climbed up on the huge back of this great white bear, and the bear slipped and slid on the ice. It finally asked, "What have you done?"

"I cut the hair from between your toes, great bear," the girl replied. "So now that you cannot chase me, why don't you take me where I want to go?"

"Where *do* you want to go?" asked the bear.

The gentle girl answered, "To the hole in the ice where you catch fish."

The big bear obliged, and soon they had caught enough fish to feed the entire village for a week. Everyone cheered as the girl rode the bear back to the village.

An elder of the village saw that the little girl had tamed the great bear, and he smiled knowingly. Someone asked him, "What has happened here?"

"Strength works best," the old man replied, "when it is harnessed with gentleness."

That big, gnarly bear illustration isn't all that difficult to apply to dads like you and me. Just because we have the upper hand with more strength, more years of experience, and more volume in our voices, doesn't mean we have the right to win every argument with our kids by *sheer force*.

The strength of fatherhood always works best when it is harnessed with gentleness. It takes a truly strong man to temper his temper with a gentle response, the same way you temper the power of a big truck with a light touch on the gas pedal.

My own father demonstrated that harnessed-bear kind of gentleness the day I drove a white, 1960 Ford pickup truck to high school.

At the time I had my eye on a cute little flute player who sat in the front row during band. Jeanie was fourteen and claimed to have "vast experience" driving a stick shift. I figured one way to impress a fourteen-year-old girl would be to let her drive "my" truck around the school parking lot. Jeanie became very excited about the possibility. I became very excited that she had become very excited. What a wonderful way to flood sunshine on a blossoming relationship.

Only two problems existed with this arrangement.

First, "my" truck actually belonged to my dad. Second, the only thing "vast" about the girl's experience with stick shifts was the size of her imagination. Her actual logged *experience* with a stick shift, it turned out, amounted to one quick drive in somebody's VW Bug.

After my hasty explanation of which pedal did what, she followed my instructions and pushed in the clutch, extending her short little left leg as far as it would go. With her toes trembling, she held that pedal down.

With her other foot, she gently pressed on the gas pedal.

The old truck roared to life as she turned the key. As I had explained, she began slowly lifting up on the clutch with her left foot while at the same time slowly depressing the gas pedal with her right foot.

That's when the plan began to unravel.

Her footwork became a bit erratic when the clutch engaged and the truck lurched forward. She tried to cram her foot back down on the clutch pedal but forgot about her right foot, which was jammed down as hard as she could push...onto the accelerator.

Sitting in the middle of the wide seat, I watched little sections of the nearby shop-class building jerk by in the rearview mirror. I felt like a rodeo cowboy riding his first bucking bronco as the truck jerked forward in wild, untamed motions.

Trying to remain calm, I yelled, "It's okay!" Who was I kidding? With nothing to hold onto, I was lurching back and forth like wet jeans in an unbalanced spin cycle.

"Just push down on the clutch and let off the gas," I hollered above the noise of the engine, which was revving and dying in time to the jerking motions of the truck.

"Which one's the clutch?" she screamed back. I guess my lesson hadn't sunk in.

"The one on the left," I said.

"Is what?" she asked. "Which one is the brake?"

We really didn't have time for this conversation to be taking place since we were quickly running out of parking lot. Just about the time I thought to help her by grabbing the stick shift and yanking it into neutral, I noticed the chain-link fence looming dangerously close to our left and just ahead.

The fence wasn't what bothered me so much. It was the

faculty parking lot filled with cars just *beyond* the fence that really got my heart racing.

Suddenly, before I had a chance to turn the key to "off" or to grab the steering wheel and turn it toward open space, I heard the sickening sound of metal against metal. Nice, straight, shiny-aluminum poles began bending like pipe cleaners as the Ford pickup-turned-tank mowed down a healthy section of newly installed fence.

Finally, for lack of gas and momentum, the old truck stalled, and silence filled the cab. I noticed my friend's cute little legs trembling as she stood straight up on both pedals, with her knuckles white and locked onto the steering wheel.

"Well," I said, breathing for the first time in several agonizing seconds, "that wasn't so bad, for a first try."

She crawled over my lap onto the passenger side of the truck while I surveyed the damage from the window. I couldn't believe what I was looking at. The bumper of the heavy old truck was resting less than twelve inches away from the bumper of the vice principal's Buick Regal.

My heart finished the bossa nova and returned to regular rhythm again, and I decided to own up to the experience. I backed the truck into an actual parking space, thanked my young friend for a lovely time, and excused myself to the vice principal's office.

Maryvale High School in Phoenix was quite large at the time, since Trevor Brown High was still under construction to our west. So, with five thousand kids to handle, our principal, David Goodson, only dealt with really major issues like riots and gun control. The vice president, a.k.a. "No Mercy" Miller, was the guy who got to hear all the really good stories...like the one I told him.

I took full responsibility for my actions and for driving the truck into the fence, feeling a bit unsettled by the wide, silly grin on his face the whole time.

When I finished my tale of woe, Mr. Miller said, "Tell you what you do. Call this number," and he handed me a business card. On it was the name and phone number of a fence company.

"They just installed the fence you ran into...*yesterday*." My knees grew weak. It was at that very moment I realized just how fortunate I had been. If that wonderful fence hadn't been there to stop our forward progress—like a cable stopping jets on an aircraft carrier—we would have nailed Mr. M's Buick but good!

He continued, "Tell the owner what happened, and see if he'll let you pay for the damages out of your own pocket. Since this happened on private property, we won't have to call the police for an accident report."

Sigh. Ah, at that moment I could have almost kissed that man. Almost. The V.P. could have given me what I really deserved—or worse—but instead, he gently helped me learn my lesson and take responsibility for my actions. He remained absolutely calm through the entire ordeal.

I called the name on the card, and a very loud man answered, "Oh yeah, heard about that little incident." I didn't know if he was loud because he was shouting over machinery noise or if he always talked like that. "I'm a little surprised to hear from you," he shouted. "One of my installers called me with the details. Says he was able to bend back three of the four posts you knocked down. The fourth one snapped like a toothpick. Why don't you come down here to my office and pay me...oh, say, ten bucks for the pipe, and we'll be back in business."

All the way down to his office I was repeating, "Thank You, God. Oh, thank You, thank You, thank You!"

With that taken care of, I faced the most difficult part of this trial. I still had to break the news to my dad.

I parked the truck as far up in the driveway as I could, with the left front fender facing away from the house. When Dad arrived home from work, I caught him as he was stepping out of the car, so I could set the right mood.

"Hey, Dad, how was work?" I acted really friendly. Maybe a tad too friendly.

"Just fine, Son. What's up?" He must have been able to tell by the way I was shifting my weight from side to side that I was a little hyped. That and the fact that my voice was up to an E-flat.

"Well, Dad, you'll never guess what happened today at school. The funniest thing." I laughed, mostly out of pure nervous energy but also hoping he would catch it and laugh with me, at least just a little.

Using the most animated and humorous expressions I could muster, I explained in detail, from start to finish, the entire episode to my father, including the fact that the vice principal had worn that silly grin on his face the whole time I was telling him my story. Then I said, "Kinda like that one you've got on your face right now, Dad!" And I laughed some more.

He sighed, chuckled, shook his head from side to side, and then put his hand on my shoulder and said, "Let's take a look at the truck."

I tried to find enough saliva in my mouth to swallow as we walked around to the damaged fender and surveyed the scratches. They weren't that bad, considering what we'd been through that day. Those old trucks were really built. He looked at the damage, sighed one more time, and then said, "You know what happened to me and one of my brothers when I was about your age?"

Suddenly I was able to swallow. I had heard his sermons before, but I figured being "preached at" was better than some other forms of punishment he might have devised. So I acted really interested.

He said, "Your uncle and I found an old truck that belonged to our dad, your grandfather. We decided to surprise him by getting the truck down the hill, into the barn, and back into working order."

(This was getting interesting. Better than most of the sermons I'd heard before.)

"Well, it wasn't until we got the old truck rolling downhill that we made a very important discovery. There were no brakes. In this instance it wasn't a chain-link fence that stopped the truck. It was a 4-inch by 4-inch fence post."

I caught myself gawking just a bit, so I closed my mouth, which had opened as Dad revealed this compelling truth about his boyhood. Not as fearful as I was before his story, I awaited sentencing.

Dad said, "I suppose that if you sand this area, first with a coarse grit and then with a fine one, we could probably match that color pretty well with a store-bought spray and just touch it up a little. This is an old truck, after all."

It had been a hat-trick day for gentleness. Three times in one day I had not been yelled at. Not once.

First the vice principal, then the man at the fence place,

and now my dad. I almost couldn't believe this was happening.

I followed Dad's advice, and in no time at all we had the old truck back in nearly good-as-used shape. The whole day had been a terrific learning experience for me: telling the truth to the vice principal, paying for the fence, helping with the bodywork on the truck, and all the while absorbing an even more valuable lesson in the process.

I learned that day about gentleness and about teaching lessons to sons who make mistakes. Dad's message sank in deep because he combined strength with gentleness. The gentleness softened the shell around my heart and allowed the arrow of truth to pierce right into its target.

One Saturday afternoon, a few weeks after I had taken his truck with me to fencing lessons, Dad was out in the driveway cleaning out the trunk of his Chevy Nova. When I walked by, he said simply, "You might want to take it easy around those curves from now on, Son."

I thought, *Does he have spies out checking my driving habits? How does he know I've been fishtailing around curves?*

Later it dawned on me. He kept a cardboard box filled with tools in the trunk of his car. I must have tipped over the box and sent tools flying. Here it was again, another one of Dad's quiet messages, gently delivered, getting the point across loud and clear.

I took it easier around the curves.

If he had jumped all over my case, I might have rebelled. But because he combined strength with gentleness, his point stuck as surely as super glue will bond your fingers together.

Whether it's found in a briefcase, a truck bed, or a car trunk, at the heart of every great father you'll find gentleness...kindly cooperating with strength.

CHAPTER THREE

At the Heart of Every Great Father
You'll Find Faithfulness

———◦◦◦———

The sound of crunching metal and breaking glass yanked me from my daydream a millisecond before the impact catapulted my head into the ceiling of the car.

Tenderly touching the bump on the top of my head, I sat in stunned silence for a moment, wondering if Linda was going to get into trouble for crashing my dad's station wagon.

My parents had driven two and a half hours south to Tucson for a two-day conference, and Linda and Mary were in charge of my sister Kathey and me. Linda, an enthusiastic, bright, fun-loving student at Grand Canyon College, and her cousin and roommate, Mary, decided to treat us kids to some ice cream after my violin lesson. (Don't let it get around that I actually took violin lessons when I was in the fourth grade. It would spoil my tough-guy reputation.)

We had gasped and laughed as "The Mountain," aptly named for the volcanolike pile of scooped ice cream, was delivered by our young, bow-tied waiter to our marble-topped table at Mary Coyles, the best place in central Phoenixi, to celebrate recitals, good report cards, and other world-class achievements.

We downed as much of the ice cream as we could hold, but ice cream makes you thirsty, so we each guzzled about three glasses of ice water and then sloshed to my folks' 1957 Chevy wagon for the ride back home. I wondered at the time if I should go to the bathroom before leaving. *Nah*, I thought. *It's a short trip.*

Linda climbed behind the wheel, Mary shouted, "Shotgun!" and got in the passenger's seat up front, and my sister Kathey put dibs on the backseat as I crawled over it into the roomy "very back" where I could sprawl out and shoot pretend laser rays at the cars behind me. I was glad my folks had driven the Rambler to their convention and left us the station wagon. It was like a good old friend.

The familiar sights of Encanto Park and Spanish-tiled roofs provided a feeling of comfort and tranquillity, especially at dusk, when this favorite part of our fair city was awash with pink-and-purple pastels and when the skyline buildings began to twinkle as they did on the opening video shots of the ten o'clock news.

Out the rear window I could tell that our car had turned off Thomas Road onto a residential street I didn't recognize, although it looked like every other residential street in that neighborhood, with rows of similarly shaped, single-story, stucco tract houses and palm trees shooting into the sunset sky. I recalled Mary saying something to Linda about picking up a term paper and a night class, so I assumed she was going to her friend's house before heading to the college to drop Mary off. Then we'd cruise south to Indian School Road and west to

Fifty-Fifth Avenue and our house, where we would watch a little television before bedtime!

As I felt the car come to a stop, I scooted around, facing forward to see where we were headed and to ask how long it would be until we got to a house with a bathroom in it. Then a sudden explosion of sound jolted me from my imaginary laser wars. We had been hit, I realized, not by a ray gun, but by an actual car in a real intersection.

Kathey *whumped* against her seat belt and was jerked back against the seat, and Linda and Mary were jostled around, but thanks to their seat belts, they didn't appear to be badly hurt. Just scared half to death.

My sister groaned and held her right side, and I felt the only thing resembling a visible injury—a bump on the top of my head.

Linda asked, to nobody in particular, "Where did that car come from?" None of us remembered seeing the lights of that stealth auto before it silently drifted through the intersection, becoming visible only when it tagged the front left fender of our Chevy with its right front fender.

Instinctively I checked my violin case to make sure the instrument was okay. Mom would kill me if I broke it. Next I looked around to see where we were. The cars were jammed against each other, smack-dab in the middle of a neighborhood intersection, just across the street from an elementary school playground. We all crawled out of the car to survey the situation as steam rose from the front.

Mary hovered over Kathey, who complained of a sharp pain on the right side of her abdomen. Linda's hand shook as she felt the bump on my head, asking, "Are you okay, kiddo? You're not bleeding, are you?"

"I'm fine," I said. "Wow. Look at the *car!*" I pointed to the radiator water, leaking out onto the pavement in a growing greenish puddle. I crossed my legs, feeling the weight of Mary Coyle's ice cream, wondering if I would be able to keep from making a puddle of my own.

Linda looked at the water on the street and groaned, feeling the weight of responsibility for this accident. This was obviously not something for which she and Mary were prepared on this fun weekend with the kids.

A kind woman had hurried over from the house across the street from the schoolyard and heard me groan from the discomfort growing in my bladder. Guiding me gently with her hands on my shoulders, she offered, "Why don't you sit down here on the curb, little man, until someone can come check you out." Then, to Linda and the driver of the other car she said, "I've called the police. They should be here in just a couple of minutes."

I had been so preoccupied with the damage to the cars that I hadn't noticed how weak my knees had become. Mumbling a feeble "Thank you," I backed up and sat on the sun-scorched yellow-brown grass between the curb and the sidewalk, watching a small parade of curious neighbors stream down the sidewalk. Between the adults on foot and the kids on bikes, we gathered a good-sized, gawking crowd.

My head throbbed a little but really no worse than from other bumps I had received from friends playing football in my own front yard. I was really more concerned about Linda and how bad she felt about the damage to our car than I was about the damage to my noggin. I didn't want her to get into trouble. She was such a nice baby-sitter. And besides, it wasn't her fault.

The action increased when a new, white Chevy Impala with a Phoenix Police Department emblem on the front door arrived, lights flashing. The lone officer spoke into his radio microphone and then unfolded his six-foot-plus frame out of the car, looking at each person to determine if any of us needed immediate attention.

One by one he approached us, asking first if we were okay and then questioning what we had seen just before the accident.

I sat, rocking slowly back and forth, legs crossed, while the officer in the sharp, navy-blue uniform jotted notes on a little pad. He had really shiny shoes. I told him, "I didn't see the other car's lights before we crashed." I paused while he wrote some more. Then I said, "I remember our car stopping at that stop sign over there before going forward again. Then, right after we started to go…WHAM!" That much I knew, since it was during the stop that I had turned around and faced forward.

I thought maybe he could help me with my more immediate problem, and I had nearly worked up enough courage to ask where a kid suffering from a leaky radiator of his own could find a bathroom when he turned, still looking at his notepad, and walked slowly toward the other side of the street, murmuring, "Thank you. Now, sir, were you the driver of the other car?"

I sighed, squeezed my legs a little tighter, and waited.

Determining that our car was in no shape to be driven, the policeman radioed for a tow truck. I heard him say to Linda, "Just to be safe, I think you'd better get to a hospital for observation. I'm a little concerned about the way the young lady keeps holding her side. If they say you're okay, then you can go home. I'll call for an ambulance. Is there someone you can call to pick you up at the hospital?"

Hospital! Ambulance! This was turning into a really cool adventure. I had *never* ridden in an ambulance before! Not even a few months earlier when I had broken my arm on the playground at school. I had thought for sure I would get to ride in an ambulance that time since my right arm was bent between my elbow and wrist so it looked like I had grown a second elbow. But the school nurse had simply taped my deformed arm to a piece of cardboard and called my grand-father, who had driven me in the Rambler—which he later sold to my parents—from the school to the hospital and then over to the "kid bone doctor." My parents had been away on a short trip that time, too, and Mom had hurried all the way home from her meeting and then across to the east side of town just in time to watch the doctor set my arm and apply the old-fashioned wet plaster cast. I think by now they were skittish about leaving us to go on trips.

By the time the tow truck and ambulance arrived, their emergency lights really lit up the neighborhood, since night had sneaked up on us. I was helped up and into the back end of the ambulance where I noticed all kinds of neat-looking medical gadgets. The attendant didn't make me lie down or attempt to give me an IV or anything, so I sat on the little bed-like gurney and queried casually, "They don't have any restrooms in these things, do they?"

No such luck. Even though we weren't bleeding or con-vulsing, I hoped these guys planned to drive really fast.

At Baptist Hospital over on Bethany Home Road, close to

Chris-Town Mall, we sat in a row of chairs in the hallway just outside an emergency-room-admitting window, where Linda and Mary nervously answered tons of questions asked by the stern-looking lady who peered authoritatively over little half-glasses that she kept perched way down on her nose. Kathey was ushered behind a curtain in the emergency room where I heard them say, "Here?" and she replied, "Ouch, yes."

Finally, almost two hours after Mary Coyles's mountain of ice cream and river of ice water had carved their way indelibly into my memory, I encountered someone who attended to my most pressing physical need.

The attending doctor busied himself by looking at my eyes with a flashlight, making my legs kick with a little rubber hammer, and instructing me to touch my fingers together in front of my face. As he performed these perfunctory functions, he asked me if I hurt, where I hurt, and how I hurt, so he could determine why I hurt. He noticed that I winced as he palpated my lower abdomen, and because I had confessed to a bout with blood in my urine a year earlier, he gave the familiar medical, "Hmmm."

Finally, he asked the most important question of the evening. "Young man," he said with a doctoral air of authority, "you are looking quite good, but I'm afraid I'm going to have to do just one more little test. Do you think it would be possible for you to give me a little urine sample in this?" and he held up a large clear flask, with c.c. measurement markers on the side.

I grinned, sighed, grabbed the flask, and asked, "How much d'ya want, Doc? Have you got two of these things?" He laughed and ushered me to a nearby restroom.

Linda returned from a pay phone where she had called the college, and she reported, "Our dorm mother said we should go back to the college tonight instead of to your house so she can keep an eye on your sister. They're a little worried about her appendix. A friend of ours is coming to pick us up." Twenty minutes later, feeling much less shaky (and ever so much lighter), I climbed into an old Ford Galaxy 500, and we headed for Grand Canyon College.

I wondered how Mom would react to the news about our little accident—especially the part about the hospital. She was the dean of women at the college, and one of her responsibilities included supervising the dorm mothers. Linda and Mary were Mom's student secretaries, so they were all tied pretty closely together.

On the ten-minute ride across Bethany Home Road to Thirty-Fifth Avenue and down to Camelback Road, Linda said, "You guys can hang out in our room tonight. Our dorm mom tried to contact your parents at the convention, but there was no way to reach them directly, so she said she'd call them at their motel after the convention is over tonight."

I was ushered in by my older sister, who had visited this dorm before. Girls were everywhere, chatting with great animation with boys in the little reception area, reading magazines or schoolbooks, watching TV in the living-room-sized lounge. Everywhere you looked, it was girls, girls, girls. Yuck.

We walked up a flight of stairs to the second story of this long, brick building named Bright Angel Hall, and when we walked through the door onto the upstairs floor, Mary yelled, "Man in the hall!"

I looked behind me, trying to catch a glimpse of the visiting dignitary who was evidently gracing us with his presence.

Kathey laughed, slapped me on the arm, and said, "She means *you*, silly."

"Oh," I said and wondered what strange customs were adopted in these foreign countries known as girls dorms.

Doors slammed, girls squealed, a couple of young ladies poked their heads around the corner and giggled, and I walked through the valley of vanity, past the smells of popcorn and fingernail polish, bravely running the gauntlet of girl-ville, to the door at the far end of the building and the relative safety of Linda and Mary's room.

It was there I finally drifted off to sleep, tucked into a makeshift bed, which was actually a mattress thrown on the floor, thinking about violin cases and radiator fluid, a policeman's shiny shoes and ambulance rides, fingernail polish, and popcorn...

I heard familiar voices and thought I was dreaming—about my parents. But what were my parents doing in a girls dorm? Dreams are weird.

But the voices sounded so real that I fluttered open my eyes, and sure enough, there, in the predawn darkness, were the unmistakable shapes of my father and mother, tiptoeing their way into the room where their two kids lay sleeping.

The dorm mother had indeed reached my mother and father late that night at their motel and had told them we were just fine. She had urged them to stay for the closing session the next day, but Mom and Dad had decided they needed to come home immediately, so they had checked out and had begun the drive back to Phoenix in the middle of the night.

Mom has always been kind of mushy, so I wasn't surprised at her reaction. She always hugged—a lot—and rarely shied away from showing her emotions. I acted tough, keeping up the macho image of boyhood while she hugged and cried and asked me three times if I was okay.

But it was Dad's reaction that caught me off guard.

While Mom was the feeler, he was the thinker. Dad was the logical, analytical, practical engineer. With slide-rule accuracy, Dad would weigh the facts, assess the situation, arrive at the best solution, and steadily go about solving the current problem.

But when my dad finally made his way over to me, he wrapped his arms around me, picking me right up off the floor, and held on tightly...for a long time. And I noticed he was doing something I had hardly ever noticed him do before.

He was crying.

Really crying. Not sobbing or moaning. No wails or sniffles. But his strong shoulders shook ever so slightly, and a drop of water fell onto my shoulder. I felt it. I knew what it was, but I couldn't remember ever feeling one of those from his face before.

He didn't say much. He just held me. And I hugged him back and relaxed in his arms. Everything was okay. Dad had shown up.

When Dad showed up for my sister and me, it was a strong, silent reminder that he cared about us. I found out just how much he cared a couple of days after our accident.

While sitting at our kitchen table, looking at Kathey's bruised side and being grateful it was just a seat belt bruise and not a ruptured appendix, Mom said, "You guys weren't the only ones to get a visit from a policeman that night."

Dad rolled his eyes and chuckled. He nodded his head up and down and then side to side, a faint look of remorse crossing his face. Kathey and I couldn't wait to hear why he was squirming.

Mom said, "He was in such a hurry to get back to Phoenix and see if you two were okay...he got a *speeding* ticket!

I thought, *No way! In that little Rambler?*

You would have to know how proud my dad was of his lifelong, unblemished driving record to understand how difficult that must have been for him. He really prided himself on safe driving, and when he saw someone driving too fast, he'd say, "That knucklehead! Must be headin' to a fire somewhere."

There were very few things that would cause my father to drive faster than the posted speed limit.

I jotted down a mental note: "My dad places a higher value on his kids' well-being than he does on his good driving record."

That was pretty high.

Years later I noticed a little verse in Psalms that reminded me how high a faithful father values his kids. "Your love," said the psalmist, "...reaches to the heavens, your faithfulness to the skies" (Psalm 36:5).

My father's faithfulness reached pretty high the night he got a speeding ticket making his way home to his kids. Not only did he show up to show he cared, but he broke one of his own rules to get there. The moment I heard about his speeding ticket, I knew without a doubt that my dad cared about us.

———◦◦◦———

That incident became the first of many that revealed to me that faithful dads show up for their kids. A father's presence at the most crucial events in his kids' lives communicates, "I care about you more than I care about the other stuff I could be doing right now."

That's one huge part of faithfulness. Showing up.

When I was in the baseball stage of life—ages nine, ten, and eleven—I'd do my homework on the kitchen table and wait for my dad to come home from work. [Then when I'd hear his old wooden swivel chair in his office squeak,] I'd stick my head around the door and ask, "Wanna play some catch?" Some days he'd say, "I can't right now, son, but I promise I'll throw the ball with you later," but more often than not, he'd push his chair back, leave his desk, and grab a mitt. He showed up for me at the simple events, like throwing a ball back and forth in the backyard. It may have only been fifteen minutes at a stretch, but they were important minutes to me.

When I got the lead in the school play my senior year of high school, I knew I could get through the nervousness of performing in front of a thousand people, because I knew my mom and dad would be sitting out there. I can't tell you what a confidence booster it was just to have my parents show up.

In college, when I'd play trombone in a concert, I'd look out across the audience, and there would be my mom and dad, looking proud. It meant a lot to me that Dad showed up.

Band concerts, violin recitals, and school plays might not be on the top-ten list of things men want to do with their spare time, but in our family, Dad showed up for nearly every performance I ever had. He did the same for my sister.

He proved his faithfulness.

He showed up.

Faithful dads not only show up for their kids, they also stand up for them.

One October when my dad was working at the Arizona Public Service Company's Buckeye office, our family drove the thirty-three miles west of Phoenix to the annual Safflower Festival, a big deal for a small farming town.

Dad had been working on a project installing gas engines used to pump huge quantities of water from desert wells to irrigation ditches so the farmers could irrigate their safflower and cotton fields. His job was partially responsible for the crops grown out there, so he wanted us to see all the products they made practically in our own backyard.

The long, narrow town of Buckeye rerouted traffic from the main highway that ran through its half-mile-long downtown, and the festival committee had closed off the four blocks at either end so they could turn their main street into an outdoor mall with booths and food stands on either side of the street.

People were free to walk back and forth across the street before and after the festival parade, and afterward they opened the highway again for travelers heading west to Los Angeles.

On the way back to our car, I tore out between two booths and across what had been a safe street moments before, not realizing the highway was now open for business. It was a stupid thing to do since a car was barreling into town at well above the posted fifty-five miles an hour.

About halfway across, I began to realize that I should have held my horses, because the horses in that car's engine were running a lot faster than I was. Both my parents hollered, "Clark! Stop!"

I did, but right in the middle of the street. Frozen in panic.

The driver laid on his brakes and left a long pair of black marks leading right up to me. My parents stood in horror as they watched the car slide quickly to where I was standing, wide-eyed and petrified, seeing the grille of this big, old car come closer and closer. It finally stopped, about two feet away.

With the look on his face, I thought my dad was preparing to spare not the rod and spoil not his child. Instead, he grabbed me by the shoulders, placed me safely behind him, and started yelling at the driver of that car, whose window was rolled down.

"Do you have any idea how fast you were going?" he shouted.

I was absolutely stunned. I had never heard my dad shout at a total stranger like that! He was always the perfect gentleman, willing to settle differences by gently talking out the issues. But now...he was really letting loose.

The man's wife sat in the passenger's seat, looking horrified, while my mother stood behind my father, looking equally horrified.

Dad stood as tall as his 5'10" frame could stretch, red faced and angry, listening as the man shouted back, "Well, your son ran out in front of *me!*"

Dad countered, "Well, *you* should drive more carefully! Didn't you see all the people milling around?"

The man came back at him, "Well, *you* should teach *your* son..."

My dad interrupted, "Well, I'll teach *YOU* a thing or..."

And before Dad could finish whatever he was about to say or do, the driver hit the gas and tore off, leaving another pair of black streaks in the road only inches away from Dad's toes and leading east toward Phoenix, away from the scene of one of the most memorable lessons I've ever lived through.

I learned that you never, *ever* run across the street without looking both ways. But more than that, I learned that my dad, who hardly ever raised his voice at anyone, stood up to that man in my defense, even though I had done a stupid thing.

I made another mental note: "My father cares enough about me to stand up in my defense, even though I'm the one at fault."

This lesson from a near accident and the one from the real accident with Linda and Mary revealed to me that faithful dads show up and stand up. They show up for their kids at important events, and they stand up on their behalf.

Faithful dads also stay put. When I think of faithfulness as it applies to a father, I think of a dad who shows up for his kids, stands up on their behalf, and stays put with their mother.

The year before my Granddaddy Hardcastle died, he told me a story about himself and a buddy way back when he was building cottages on an island in Oak Creek Canyon,

Arizona—the same island where I would later spend a summer helping him build a house.

Granddaddy said, "My friend and I were walking along the creek, near the little building we called the Honeymoon Cottage, when a couple of ladies walked up to us. One woman put her hand on her hip, looked at me, and said, 'I'll take this little feller, and you can have the other one.' And then she gave a Betty Davis look and asked, 'Wanna come over to our place, fellas? You could have a little lunch, and afterward...' and she made a little growling sound."

Granddaddy continued, "I looked that lady right in the eyes and said, 'I've been happily married to one woman for years now, and she's sittin' right over *that* hill waitin' for me to come home and eat the lunch she's made for me. I plan to eat *that* lunch, and I plan to stay married to *that* woman.'"

That's faithfulness.

Granddaddy celebrated seventy-two wedding anniversaries with the woman who made him that lunch and several thousand other lunches.

He felt compelled to share that story after I was married and had three kids of my own. I guess he wanted to demonstrate that a commitment-based, fidelity-type faithfulness is still possible even though it might not be fashionable.

I got his point. I have remained faithful to my lovely wife, Joy, though quite honestly our marriage hasn't always been easy. We're learning that faithfulness is fidelity dressed in overalls; it takes a lot of work—but it's well worth it.

It's that kind of faithfulness that helps me respect both my grandfather and my dad even more. They remained faithful to God, to their respective wives, and to their kids. That kind of faithfulness communicates, "I think you're important enough to remain pure and committed to you. I value your relationship more than any other."

Both Granddaddy and Dad modeled faithfulness as fathers. They showed up, stood up, and stayed put. And that was no accident. They stayed faithful on purpose, completing one little faithful act after another.

Oh yes, speaking of accidents, I forgot to tell you what happened to our '57 Chevy wagon. The accident with Linda and Mary finally did the old car in. Dad was sad to say good-bye to the old faithful friend, but he said, "It's just a car. I'm glad you kids are okay. People matter a lot more than a hunk of metal."

We also found out that Dad's insurance company investigated the other driver and uncovered several other accidents in his past. Apparently, this guy had sued several people for injuries he had never sustained. The insurance company concluded that he might have had his lights off on purpose, so he could drive into an oncoming car from a side street and then file a claim for an outrageous injury.

Thanks, Dad, for going easy on Linda and for showing up for us, for standing up on our behalf, and for staying put with Mom. It was no accident that you remained a faithful father.

CHAPTER FOUR

At the Heart of Every Great Father
You'll Find Goodness

———⟞⟨⟩⟞———

B lood was everywhere."
My brother-in-law, Chris Pollard, shook his head as he told the story. Months had passed since his little girl's surgery, but he was still visibly shaken by its retelling. Chris is a man's man, but when it comes to his kids, he's a true tender warrior.

"Lynsey started bleeding after we got her home from the hospital. The doctor said we could expect a *little* bleeding, but we knew something was really wrong."

Bad tonsils are common, but every so often after a typical operation, a rare complication sets in. This was unfortunately true in Lynsey's case. Her parents prayed as they rushed her back to the hospital, where the doctor met them.

"Even the doctor was upset by the amount of blood Lynsey was losing. He tried to stop it, and after working for about two minutes with no success, he had to walk away for a few seconds to get a grip. I was almost ready to grab him and say, 'Hey, my daughter's over there bleeding! Don't fall apart *now!*' But he took a deep breath and went back to try again."

After what seemed an eternity, the doctor succeeded in clamping off the bleeding artery in Lynsey's throat. He wiped the sweat from his forehead and smiled at the trembling little girl who appeared as white as the paper she was lying on.

"There you are, sweetie. You're as good as new." He was as relieved as she was.

Still covered with the crimson reminder of her frightening ordeal and barely able to speak, the petite patient flashed a weak smile back at the doctor and croaked, "Thank you."

Hardly able to speak himself, the doctor leaned over, gently hugged little Lynsey, and said, "Oh, honey, you are extraordinary."

How in the world was Lynsey able to offer such kind words to the one who had inflicted such pain? I think it's because she knew the doctor was doing for her what she needed for her ultimate good.

The doctor's actions provide a fitting working definition of the word *goodness*: giving to someone what will lead to his or her ultimate benefit. He demonstrated goodness by doing the right thing for Lynsey, even though it was temporarily painful and terribly uncomfortable. And Lynsey's dad, Chris, did the right thing by taking Lynsey to the doctor in the first place.

Would he have been a good dad if he had said, "Ah heck, let's just keep her at home. It's only blood. I don't want that old doctor to hurt her anymore"?

Of course not. Chris demonstrated goodness as a dad because he did what was best for his daughter—even though it was painful at the time.

I stumbled onto an example of my dad's goodness when my preteen, slightly elevated degree of obsession with two-wheel transportation broke into full-blown minibike fever.

The newspaper's want ads had disappointed me for weeks—ever since I had been watching the minibike market for highs and lows, hoping to find some family as eager to sell as I was eager to buy. It was the Great Depression for me because minibikes were climbing way too high in price.

A downturn in price finally turned up my enthusiasm level when I saw a little two-line advertisement that said simply, "Minibike. 5 horse Briggs and Stratton. $50," and included a phone number.

That was all the description my one-track, two-wheel mind needed to start its campaign.

"Dad," I began, after he returned from work that evening, "I found a really good buy on a minibike, and I can afford it with the money I've been saving from picking up trash in the parking lots of fast-food restaurants and helping Kent with his paper route. Can we go look at it?"

Dads are often put in tough situations. I'm discovering that fact now that my kids are old enough to come up with plans like the one I used on my father.

We dads are used to hearing sales pitches every day, and he knew some of them are just nearly impossible to say no to. That's what I had counted on, and since I had practiced my speech, eliminating every possible objection before my father had a chance to raise it, I just knew there would be very little discussion before I got what I wanted—a trip to the house where this wonderful family was willing to part with a fantastic minibike at a ridiculously low price, probably so a well-behaved kid like me would have the joy of riding with the wind in his hair and dirt in his teeth.

The wheels turned in my dad's head, and he arrived at the first objection. It was the old safety factor (often used to stall when dads don't know what else to say). "Well, Son," he said, rubbing his five o'clock shadow, "where would you ride this piece of machinery? It's not a toy, you know." (I had known he would say that, including the part about not being a toy. He was playing right into my hands.)

"Oh, I would *never* ride it on the road!" I replied with great sincerity. I was covered for this contingency. The well-rehearsed words rolled off my tongue like *thees* and *thous* from a Shakespearean actor. "We could take it down to the junior high school parking lot. That's where Kent's dad takes him. Or out into the desert, up near Bell Road, off the freeway. They've got lots of dirt trails there and a few small hills to climb. Nothing really dangerous though." Scene One had gone quite well.

He nodded, obviously weighing my argument for safety.

"And what about a helmet?"

I had practiced for this scene, too. "Kent just bought a new one, and he said he'd sell me his used one for five bucks." (I had learned it was better to say what I needed to say quickly and then just stop. The more I talked, the more I put my foot in my mouth, and it sounded like I was trying too hard. So I just recited my lines, paused, waited, and prayed.)

"I suppose we could take a look at it…" (Yes! I knew I had

won already, and after only two possible objections) "...on one condition."

Ooohh. The "one condition." Those pesky small-print items thrown in at the last minute—like the tax on jellybeans thrown into the national budget at 11:59 P.M. the night before Congress is scheduled to adjourn.

There's *never* a way to plan ahead for the "one condition," and I fretted briefly about what it would be.

That I clean my room every day? Mow the lawn every week, without complaining? Haul out the trash for the next ten years? I'd do it—I'd do it *all* if I had to—for a minibike's sake. If that's what it was going to take, then frankly, Scarlet...I'd do it!

"I'll take you to see it," Dad continued, "*if* you promise me that *if* you buy it—and I'll need to look it over to see if it's okay *before* we buy it—that you will *not* ride it unless I'm around to supervise. What do you say? Deal?"

Every good salesman knows when to close the sale. "Deal!" I said quickly. "When can we go? Now?" It sounded too good to be true. What a simple condition. Sure, I could wait until my dad was around to supervise. Why not? He would give me plenty of opportunities to ride. No problem.

He shifted his glance, looked at his watch, sighed, then looked back at his watch. I knew he was thinking that I was thinking that the minibike would surely be gone if we waited until tomorrow to go see it. After all, it was *only* fifty bucks. There were probably three potential buyers on their way out the doors of their houses at this very moment.

"I've got a meeting to go to at seven, so *if* we go right now..."

It was looking hopeful, but the *if* bothered me. One more *if* and I would stop breathing.

"...we would get back just in time for me to take off for the meeting, which means you'd have to put it up and not ride it until Saturday when I could be there to supervise. Okay?"

I was already on my way out the door.

An hour and a half later we were pulling into the driveway, the proud owner of the "new" minibike hanging out the passenger's side window of the station wagon, grinning from ear to ear.

As my dad helped me yank the little machine out into open air, my buddies from three houses in either direction and one from across the street all came running.

"Wow!" "Neato," "Cool," "Awesome," and "How fast does it go?" came buzzing out of five mouths simultaneously.

"Uh, I dunno. But isn't it great?"

They inspected the centrifugal clutch, a new term I threw around like I'd been a minibike mechanic for years. They pressed on the mechanical brake, which meant a steel rod that ran to a welded steel plate that rubbed against the back tire. They looked at the little shock absorber ingeniously engineered into the front fork, providing the appearance of a midget Harley Hog. An ugly Harley, yes, but a Harley nonetheless.

My dad looked at me and smiled as he saw how excited my friends were to see my used-but-new-to-me, actually motorized, two-wheel vehicle. I had arrived home with new status in the neighborhood.

He said with that semi-stern voice dads reserve for making their point but showing that they still care about you, "Remember our deal," and then patted me on the shoulder and headed for the house to gather his stuff to take to the meeting at seven.

Oh yeah. The meeting. Oooh I couldn't *wait* until Saturday. I wondered how fast that thing would go. Would it do a wheelie? Would I be able to jump six cars and a pickup truck by hurtling up a ramp? Man, I bet it would go forty, fifty, maybe sixty miles an hour, at least maybe down a really steep hill.

Kent said, "Fire it up, and let's hear how she runs!"

"I can't. I'm not supposed to ride it until my dad can watch me."

"Oh."

Gavin joined the quest for a minibike exhibition. "Well, how about if we just push you around the yard?"

"Yeah. Okay. That's not really *riding* it...I guess."

They pushed and I steered. Whew, it was glorious. I couldn't wait to feel what it would be like when the little monster actually propelled itself.

"Couldn't you just let it run for a second—so we could hear the engine?" Gavin suggested. His full name was Gavin "Take it to the limit" Henderson.

"Yeah, it wouldn't be like you were really *riding* it," chimed in Kent's little brother, P.D. His name was Paul Dean, but we all called him P.D.

"Well..." I hesitated.

By then Kent was already yanking on the pull rope, and Gavin was fiddling with the gas valve, turning it to "on."

It did sound reasonable. I mean, after all, I wouldn't actually ride it across the yard or anything. I'd just let it idle, to hear the sound of all that harnessed power.

"Man, just listen to that thing," shouted Kent over the noise of the little lawn-mower engine.

"How does the clutch work?" P.D. hollered in my ear.

"Like this," I said, feeling the vibration of man on machine, and then just twisted the throttle back a tiny bit on the right handlebar. The little clutch spun around a little faster as the engine sped up, and suddenly the minibike was moving, ever so slowly, across the front yard toward the driveway. I was caught up in the moment. It was exhilarating.

That's when my father walked out the front door.

Oops.

He looked at me, took in a long, deep breath, looked up at the sky, rolled his head to one side, closed his eyes, and just stayed like that for five agonizing seconds as he exhaled v-e-r-y slowly.

I could tell he was thinking, hard. I shut the engine off and sat there, wondering what he would say. It was obvious that this decision was killing him as much as it was killing me.

"Son, you know as much as I hate to do this…"

Oh man. I knew what was coming, because we had just discussed our "deal" in the car. A week! One entire *week*. Seven interminable days. That's how long we had agreed the minibike would remain on the patio *if* (and I *had* agreed to the "if" clause) I ever violated the terms of its probation.

"…I'm afraid I *have* to ask you to put the minibike on the patio. You made a deal."

Ugh. Shoot. Darn. Heck. Ugh again. I *knew* better. It was just so easy to get caught up in the thrill of something so new, so…exciting. But I knew better.

All my friends began looking at the ground and saying,

"See ya," "Bye," "Later," and they shuffled off toward their houses. I chewed my lower lip, nodded my head as if to say, "I understand," and pushed the silent machine into the backyard through the side gate and around to the patio, where I leaned it against the bicycle kickstand the creator/owner had welded onto the homespun frame. And I just sat down on the concrete, looking at it, wishing like crazy I hadn't ridden it across the yard.

"Stupid," I said, hitting my leg with the palm of my hand for emphasis. "Stupid, stupid, *stupid.*"

Although I was terribly disappointed by having my minibike grounded during the first ten minutes after its arrival at its new home, I did eventually have many wonderful experiences with that little thing. The first day after it was released from lockup, Dad took me down to the junior high school parking lot and let me ride until it was out of gas.

I remember watching other kids in my neighborhood in those formative years, as they took off on their motorcycles to parts unknown, at all hours of the day and night, often without their parents' permission, and I couldn't help but feel a little respect for a dad who enforced the rules. I knew it just about killed him to say no sometimes, but I also knew he was upholding the boundaries for my ultimate good.

One of my best friends ended up doing time in a Florence, Arizona, prison. Evidently the lack of respect for the boundaries in his home took its toll. It wasn't until much later, years after the minibike incident, when I truly understood that my dad was demonstrating the wonderful quality of goodness by grounding me that day.

He hated to ground me, and said so, but a deal was a deal,

and his deal was motivated out of love for me and a desire to protect me from harm. He was doing for me what would ultimately lead to my good, even though it was painful at the time. That's genuine goodness.

Fathers teach the quality of goodness to their kids when they wrestle with the question, "What is the right thing to do in this situation?"

Sometimes doing the right thing means imposing a boundary—saying no—and sometimes it means allowing a choice—saying yes. Always it means being motivated by the overall best interest of the other person.

Goodness is not always painted in black-and-white strokes. Oh sure, most of the time it's easy to tell right from wrong. Most of the time you don't even have to think about it, because right is always right, and wrong is always wrong. But once in a great while our kids will be placed in situations where it won't be quite that easy, where they will simply have to ask, "What would Jesus do?"

My dad taught me to ask that question, and one hot, August, Friday evening in Phoenix, the lessons about goodness were put to a test.

On my way to the door my eyes met with the shy, courageous eyes of the girl with the scar above her upper lip.

The quartet I was in had just performed for the "halftime show" of the United Methodist Church dance. I had fought with myself about accepting the engagement since I was plagued with my upbringing. You see, I was a Baptist.

The parallel truth to the movie title *White Men Don't Jump* is the truth *Baptists Don't Dance.*

In our Baptist world the word *dance* was pronounced "day-ance" and was said through clenched teeth with a clenched fist, as though it were synonymous with the word *sin.* (My parents didn't say it that way, but most everybody else did.)

I thought I would be able to exit quietly soon after we sang, thus avoiding the temptation to "day-ance." I was fairly certain I could sneak in, sing our half-hour set, and then slip out without so much as touching a person of the opposite—well, you know.

I was absolutely sure I wouldn't wind up outside, behind the bushes, as had so many fabled Baptist youth who had been swayed by the "jungle beat" and yielded to temptation, doing the dirty deed of, well, "day-ancing."

Before I could find the back door, though, the DJ's voice echoed off the brick walls, "Okay, girls, here's your chance. The first dance of the second half is 'girl ask boy.'" That's when the nice young lady with the scarred upper lip shyly approached, hoping to catch my eye.

She displayed the courage of a soldier as she fought fear and defeated doubt. She risked rejection and humiliation by asking me to dance.

But her eyes didn't say "day-ance." They only said "please."

It was like the time I worked up enough nerve to challenge my father to an arm-wrestling match. I was pretty sure he'd win, but I really wanted to try, if only to enjoy a few seconds of contact with someone who cared about me.

The scar on this young woman's face was not totally unattractive, yet it was not at all subtle. It had become necessary because of a slight abnormality at birth, what the cruel kids called a "harelip."

In milliseconds my mind searched for the right thing to do. My early convictions with the word *day-ance* brought only a one-word answer—*No*.

In the black-or-white, wrong-or-right culture of Baptists, it was wrong to day-ance. PERIOD. And if it was wrong yesterday, then, brother, it was wrong today, and it would be wrong tomorrow.

The only possible time it was ever okay to day-ance, I thought, was when the two people who were physically intertwined were married, and then probably they were totally embarrassed and also probably behind closed doors.

The only other thing I knew that people did when they were married, physically intertwined, totally embarrassed, and behind closed doors was—well, you know.

In fact, that pretty much summed up the linkage. You didn't do those two things—day-ancing and the other thing—until after you were married.

The two activities might as well be described with the same word. In my subconscious Baptist mind, they probably were. Say the word *day-ance,* and you've said, well, the other word.

Ah, that's the stuff of which convictions are made. Two connections from previous cultural influences, both so strong that the two are married as one conviction. And you act on those convictions without even thinking.

But then, without warning, in a moment of decision, compassion shyly walked up to conviction and gave "that look."

The eyes begged conviction to rethink its reasoning. The same eyes that, when I was six years old, had looked at my dad and said, "I know you'll probably say no, but I'm willing to risk rejection in order to gain a few seconds of being close to someone I really look up to."

When I was a kid, my dad smiled, put his right elbow on the table, extending his hand, palm open, ready to receive mine. When I was in high school, I smiled, bent my right elbow, extending my hand, palm open, so this shy, courageous girl's hand could be placed in mine.

Suddenly I was glad the lights were dimmed, since I could feel my face grow red from the embarrassment of a little shyness of my own. In that moment I believe several events from history converged into one event: The good Samaritan broke cultural tradition and stooped down to tend the wounds of a beaten, forgotten man on a lonely dirt road...a leper courageously stepped across the social "do not cross" yellow plastic tape...and a woman caught in adultery looked up through tear-filled eyes to an empty street after Jesus had proclaimed, "Let the sinless one cast the first stone."

I couldn't imagine being stoned for dancing with this gentle girl. But I had no doubt that a jury of dyed-in-the-wool, cultural Christians would have convicted me, the same way a jury of hypocritical Pharisees condemned Jesus for healing on the Sabbath, or touching a leper, or talking with a prostitute.

But a jury of genuine believers, those who had been touched by the goodness felt in the healing hand of Jesus Himself, would never have found me guilty. They would have pronounced the word *dance,* not *day-ance.*

This touch was not sensual. It was healing. In milliseconds my mind concluded, *In this case, for you NOT to dance would be sin.*

When I was a kid, my dad took me up on my request. He let me put my hand in his, and he let me win. I felt a surge of healing gratitude when my little hand thumped down on the dining room table with his big hand underneath. Mercy had just overpowered judgment.

When I was in high school, I left that fellowship hall after only one dance. It was the dance reserved for the shy, courageous girl with the somewhat attractive little scar over her upper lip.

And as I walked outside under the warm summer sky, at exactly the same moment the door shut behind me I could hear the solid thump of conviction's big hand hitting the table.

Goodness had won out. Compassion had just beaten conviction. Mercy had triumphed over judgment.

Genuine, compassionate, fathering goodness, I discovered, means doing what will result in our children's ultimate good, even though it seems tough at the time.

Jesus, teaching about His Father's goodness, said, "Which of you, if his son asks for bread, will give him a stone? Or if he asks for a fish, will give him a snake?" (Matthew 7:9–10).

Modern translation? The heavenly Father gives to His kids what will result in their ultimate good, even if it means giving them boundaries (saying no once in a while) or allowing choices (saying yes once in a while). He will *never* give them what is bad for them. Never.

He continued, "How much more [than the imperfect human fathers] will your Father in heaven give good gifts to those who ask him! So in everything, do to others what you would have them do to you" (7:11–12).

My dad gave me a good gift when our family watched the cap to our canteen go rolling off a rock and down a thousand-foot drop to the bottom of a canyon.

He *yelled* at me.

We were gawking at the amazing spire of Spider Rock jutting up from the canyon floor like a sandstone Empire State Building, right in the middle of Canyon DeChelly (pronounced "Da-*Shey*") in northern New Mexico. Dad had carefully instructed us to crawl, on our bellies, up to the edge and look down the sheer cliff—one thousand feet down—to the little mud-and-stick house at the bottom, where an American Indian woman was chopping wood.

We would start counting when we saw the ax blade hit the wood. One, two, three, four, five, six, seven. Then we would hear *Whack!* It was awesome. And scary. To be that high up and to reach out and touch the air that was the only thing between you and a thousand-foot fall to certain death was exhilarating—and terrifying.

Like grunts in boot camp crawling under barbed wire fence, we kept as low to the ground as possible, pushing with our elbows and knees, backing up, creeping away from the edge of the huge, flat rock that had been our observation post. That's when the cap fell off the canteen and started rolling toward the edge of the cliff. Without thinking, I made a lunge for it.

Dad yelled, *"STOP! Don't go after it!"*

He was quick, firm, very loud, and absolutely insistent. There was no time for diplomacy. Dad was as loud and assertive as Jesus must have been when he heaved over those moneychangers' tables in the temple, trying to get His point across in a way that would capture their attention.

Dad got mine.

And I thanked him for it.

How can you thank someone for yelling at you? It's easy when you know he was motivated by a deep love that wants the very best for your safety and well-being.

It seems the deeper the love and the graver the danger, the louder the yell. He was demonstrating goodness by doing for me what he knew would keep me from going over the edge. He was doing for me what he would have been grateful for someone to do for him.

That's a good way to sum up goodness—doing unto others what you would have them do to you. Sometimes it's clear-cut. Black and white. Obvious. Sometimes it means wrestling with whether to say yes or no. And it may be painful at the moment. But every time we dads do what Jesus would do, we can bet it will be the right thing.

And after the fact, because the child knows the father has acted out of genuine goodness, he or she will be able to say what little Lynsey croaked to her doctor in the emergency room.

"Thank you."

Thank you for doing the right thing.

CHAPTER FIVE

At the Heart of Every Great Father
You'll Find Kindness

━━◈◈◈◈━━

Ten-year-old Joseph Fisher learned a lesson on kindness when he almost ran over his dad with a tractor.

Dr. "Just call me Joe" Fisher is one of two very talented partners at Orion International, a management consulting firm in Ann Arbor, Michigan. Joe is outstanding in his field, helping top level leaders in major corporations make those small, midcourse corrections in their leadership that tighten the focus and keep the ship sailing to precisely the right place on the map.

One reason Joe is able to give feedback to high-performance people is because years ago he learned from his dad (a farmer who was outstanding in *his* field) how to teach leaders so they will want to learn and so the lessons will stick. Listen as Joe tells his story.

"I was breaking up some dirt one afternoon while my dad was working on a piece of equipment in the bar ditch on the north side of the field.

"The old Farmall tractor I was driving had to be turned by pulling a brake on one rear wheel or the other. If you applied the brake to the left wheel, the right wheel kept turning, so naturally, the tractor turned left. If you pulled the right brake, you turned right. It seems so obvious, but when you're ten…you sometimes forget these basic instructions.

"My dad was seated on the opposite side of the ditch, directly in front of where I was headed, and he was intent on his work, so he didn't see the big double wheels of the tractor until I pulled the wrong brake and started the tractor sliding in the wrong direction.

"I almost panicked, trying to stop the big old thing, but my dad jumped out of the way at the last minute, and the heavy front end of the tractor thumped to a stop right where Dad had been sitting.

"I expected him to come clean my plow (and not on the tractor), so I sat with my hands on the wheel, bracing myself for the explosion. Instead, he calmly walked up to me and asked, 'Are you okay?'

"I couldn't believe it. Here I was sitting on this huge tractor that I had almost steered right over my dad, and he asked if I was okay! When I told him I was fine, he simply said, 'Well, good. Do you know what you did wrong?' I told him, 'Yes sir,' and he said, 'Great. There's a lesson you won't soon forget.' And he just smiled, patted my knee, and watched me drive the tractor back onto the field. Then he climbed back into the ditch and went back to work."

Kindness, Joe discovered, has a lot to do with the fine, fatherly art of instruction.

Here was a dad who knew how to throw on the instruction so the learning sticks. He used kindness to get across his point.

I absolutely marveled at Joe's story. So many dads would have torn into their sons like disks into the dirt for almost running over them. But Joe said, "Dad's way to discipline was simply to teach me how to be responsible. He figured I had already punished myself for the blunder, and making me feel stupid for an honest mistake didn't seem to help the situation. So he simply used the teachable moment to teach, knowing that the lesson would not be forgotten."

Obviously it wasn't. That incident happened over forty years ago, yet Joe related every detail as though it happened last week.

Wise Solomon must have learned a few things about instructive kindness from his dad, David...or maybe it was from the heavenly Father who loved the young king so dearly. Solomon wrote: "Reckless words pierce like a sword, but the tongue of the wise brings healing.... The tongue that brings healing is a tree of life, but a deceitful tongue crushes the spirit" (Proverbs 12:18; 15:4).

Ken Blanchard said, "Don't punish a learner. If you do, you'll immobilize him." Joe's dad didn't punish his little learner. He kindly instructed him and helped him become responsible, just like Ron Potter did for me back when I was floundering with administrative details.

Ron called and asked if he could take me to lunch. I said, "Sure." I was always up for good food and the encouragement of someone who constantly left me feeling better than before I met with him.

He met me at Wendy's, and we exchanged weather talk and bantered about Michigan football for a few minutes. Then Ron got serious.

"Would you be offended if I gave you a gift?" he asked.

Offended? By a gift? Not unless it was the gift of a kick in the pants. Sure, why not? I told him, "Of course not," and waited as he went out to his car and brought in a small box.

As I opened the package, Ron continued, "I've noticed that you've had a little trouble with some administrative stuff at the church. Little things, like following up on phone calls that need to be made after a meeting. Stuff like that."

I pulled out a new calendar notebook, just like the one Ron used to keep his company humming. He was then the president of T&B Computing.

"Wow," I said, not knowing what else to say.

"I don't mean to tell you how to run *your* business, but I'd be happy to show you how I've organized my notebook—if you'd be interested in trying one out for yourself. Mine sure has helped me keep from dropping so many loose ends."

How can you say no to such an incredible chance to learn? He spent a good forty-five minutes answering every question I fired at him. Within two weeks, I was feeling much less stressed and much more organized at the church where I served as minister of education and music.

Ron was my mentor, deacon, and friend. Later, Ron would become a partner, along with another professional feedback giver, Joe Fisher, at Orion International. I count it a rare privilege that both Ron and Joe consider themselves my friends.

Ron did for me what Joe's father did for him. He demonstrated kindness by offering to instruct rather than seeking to punish. He could have gone behind my back and stirred up trouble, turning people against my leadership. Instead, he kindly pointed me on the right track and increased my productivity by helping me get better organized. I'm still using the planner he gave me years ago.

Ron knew the secret of effective feedback. He didn't punish the learner. He kindly instructed me, helping me to become responsible, the same way my father did with me back when my minibike fever broke out into a full-blown case of motorcycle-itis.

Something was haywire with my telepathic powers. That much concentration, that much thought projection, that much *longing* should have had some effect. But Dad just kept on driving.

Can you recall a time when, as a kid, you really—I mean *desperately*—wanted something, and you said, "I'd do just about anything to _____"?

I remember such a time. It had a lot to do with a minibike hunger that aged into a motorcycle-sized appetite. Every time my dad would drive past the Honda place on Indian School Road, across the street from K-Mart, I would cross my fingers and hold my breath, trying to transfer thoughts to my dad. My brain waves would be shouting at him, "Turn in here. Turn in *here*. Oh, Dad! You *want* to turn in *here!* Buy your son a motorcycle. Turn in here, NOW!"

Strange thing about those feeble telepathic powers. Either my transmitter batteries were dead or his receiver was busted.

He never seemed to get those invisible, inaudible hints.

Eventually, however, my dad revealed real kindness to me and helped me solve my motorcycle problem...but not in a way I expected.

Even though I thought my father had totally missed my huge hints about a dirt bike, he surprised me one evening at supper. We were sitting around the table talking family talk, just "stuff," when out of the blue he spoke up and said, "Son, your mother and I were thinking about your motorcycle problem."

He was? They were? Wow. I didn't know anyone even knew I had a "problem." I nearly dropped my fork and decided it was time to really listen up. This could be good.

Dad continued, "Your mother and I have been talking, and..."

Oh man, I was *way* ahead of him. I could just hear the words roll off his tongue, "...and we've decided to buy you that one you keep pointing at every time we drive by the shop, because you've been such a good kid..."

Wrong. Oh, the imagination can play such evil tricks on a young lad.

What he actually said was, "...and we spoke with Granddaddy about it..."

Oh, so that was it. He was going to tap into the deep pockets of my generous grandfather. How nice. It would give Granddaddy such satisfaction to know he had provided such huge fun to his grandson.

"...and he offered to let you come work..."

Work? Did I hear that word right? *Work?*

"...with him this summer since he's building their house up in Sedona."

Yes, and...?

"And with the money you earn from working as his carpenter's assistant, you should nearly be able to afford that motorcycle you've had your eye on."

Work? I was still stuck on the word that had sneaked in the backdoor of this conversation a couple of sentences ago.

"What do you think, Son?"

I was stunned. Silent. Unprepared to respond to this particular offer. It didn't fit any of the acceptance speeches I had memorized for such an occasion.

"Uh, how long would that take? To build a house I mean?"

"He tells me you should just about get it framed and get a roof on it before you have to come back down to Phoenix and start school in September."

"Oh."

I was considering my options. The motorcycle part of the deal sounded good, but a *whole summer of work*—and *then* the motorcycle? This waiting stuff seemed to be a big part of their plan.

But, hey, it was the only offer on the table! I decided to take it. It beat mowing lawns in the 110-degree desert sun.

"When do we start?" I asked.

"We can drive you up the Monday after your last day of school."

"Okay then."

And that's when the lessons on kindness really began.

—◦◦◦—

I felt really stupid wearing that dumb, blue cowboy hat, but I couldn't refuse the man who bought it for me.

As a kid, I didn't question my grandfather when he told me to do something. He was the boss.

He had *earned* the right to be boss for two reasons. First, he was fifty-two years older than I was, and I was only fourteen. You can do the math.

Second, he had learned about everything there is to learn about building a house—and not by watching *Home Improvement* either. He had built bunches of houses, from scratch, with his bare hands.

So with Granddaddy permanently planted in my mind as the boss, I was prepared to be his apprentice that summer, if for no other reason than to get that motorcycle.

The first day I arrived he drove me to a department store and said, "We need to get you a hat. Working out in the sun will fry your brains. Some days this Arizona sun comes down through a funnel! Let's see what we can find." But his idea of a hat and my idea of a hat were about as far apart as the stakes marking the corners of his lot. I pictured one of those cool, expensive hats like the country singers wore, not the blue straw, kidlike hat with that little string hanging down around your chin. Those were for babies.

But I didn't have the heart to tell him I was way too old for that sort of thing. And I reasoned that since his property was stuck off in the woods, we'd be off to ourselves and away from people most of the time, and nobody would see me wear the silly thing.

I took it off a few times when truck drivers came to the building site to deliver lumber and supplies. Then I put it back on after they'd gone. I don't think Granddaddy noticed.

Granddaddy's name was Willard. I had secretly dubbed him "Willard the Wise," because he knew absolutely everything about building. He handed out directions with gentle authority—like a benevolent ship's captain or the fatherly manager of a big league ball team. He knew what he wanted, and he knew precisely how he wanted it done.

For instance, I not only knew where to place the two, sixteen-penny nails—through the plate into the stud—but I knew how to hold the hammer, how to stand, and how to swing with maximum efficiency to drive the nails straight and with a minimum of wasted energy. Granddaddy never wasted anything. (He even went to the bathroom around the base of a little pine tree to make sure his own waste wasn't wasted.) Granddaddy elevated something as mundane as hammering to an art form.

I must have swung that hammer three times to his one, but I learned by watching, and after a couple of weeks I was bending 30 percent fewer nails. Granddaddy was very small in stature—about five feet and an inch or so—yet he could drive a nail as quickly and cleanly as some Rambo-like carpenter twice his size.

Size, or lack of it, never seemed to bother Willard the Wise.

In fact, I believe Granddaddy's size had taught him how to look for ways to do work easier, with more leverage and less brute strength. He would say, "I'm more interested in what you do with what you *have* than in complaining about what you don't have."

Until that summer my longest day of work consisted of mowing our little lawn in the city or taking out the trash. Making my bed was pretty tough, too, but I couldn't seem to convince my mother of that fact.

Each night of the first week at Granddaddy's I crawled into the shower and back out again and then slithered into bed, as tired as a hamster on a treadmill powering a cement mixer. Granddaddy's goal in life that summer was to help me appreciate what he meant when he said, "Workin' from can see till can't see."

I remember lying in bed each night, looking up at the ceiling, feeling the soft quilts and smelling the lingering fragrance of my grandmother's good cooking. *Most kids would be goofing off at this time of year,* I reminded myself as I drifted into oblivion. *Any kid can play, but THIS is WORK.*

Granddaddy's lessons on life came in little sentences, not long boring sermons, and they usually related to some skill he was showing me at the time, such as how to carry heavy things.

He'd say, "Sonny Boy (his nickname for me that summer), you'll wear yourself out tryin' to do too much too fast. Just take as much as you can easily manage, and make several trips. It'll save your back. Remember, slow and steady wins the race."

Good advice on carrying things. Good advice on life.

He taught me how to paint. "Don't scrape all your paint off your brush onto the lip of the can," he'd say, as he was showing me. "Leave enough paint on the brush to cover more completely, then you don't have to make so many strokes. And feather the edges to blend it with the previous strokes, like this…" And he'd show me a perfect style to imitate.

It's easier to learn when someone *shows* you how to do something—the right way—than it is to learn when someone just tells you about it.

Perhaps the greatest lesson I learned from my grandfather, the carpenter, was the lesson from that stupid, blue cowboy hat.

I learned that summer of my fourteenth year that kindness is a boomerang. The more effort you put into giving it away, the harder it hits when it comes back to you.

I didn't know it at the time, but Granddaddy had mourned the loss of a baby much earlier in his life. Grandmother had given birth to a baby boy who, if he had grown up, would have been my uncle. My mother and her sister were their only remaining children.

So I had no idea that this whole summer-of-work idea was not just for my motorcycle benefit. It seems I was the answer to one of Willard's lifelong dreams.

To teach a son the skills he loved.

I was the son he had always wanted. I was his "Sonny Boy."

I didn't know this until a couple of years after I spent that summer with him. One afternoon when my mother and I were having a nostalgiafest, recalling that Sedona summer, she reached into her treasure box of memories, pulled out a couple of secrets, and gave them to me as a growing-up gift.

The first gift was the knowledge about the uncle I never had and the reason Granddaddy wanted to teach me some of his favorite things.

The second secret smacked me harder than the first, like that boomerang I mentioned—cracking you in the head from behind because you don't see it coming. (Actually I have experienced that memorable sensation with a *real* boomerang. Trust me on this one, it makes an impression.)

As my mom unraveled her story, I could almost smell the sawdust and feel the splinters under my fingernails. My mind rushed back with incredible clarity to the very place where my Granddaddy found the little hat.

According to my mother, the day after I left Sedona to go back to school, my tough, not-very-emotional grandfather walked into the toolshed to start work. He spied the little blue cowboy hat hanging on a nail where I'd left it every night after work. (I wasn't about to wear it into town.)

He picked it up and ran his fingers over it, just remembering.

And as my mom finished the story, her words drove into my own heart like a hammer driving a sixteen-penny nail. She said, "Your granddaddy sat down on an overturned bucket, held that little blue hat, and cried like a baby."

How did my mother find out? I wondered. How did she gain this secret knowledge, this gift of kindness she was passing along to me as I grew into manhood?

My granddaddy had unlocked this treasured memory a year after he held the hat, and he handed the treasure to my grandmother, who later handed it to my mother. It's not the sort of confession macho carpenters are in the habit of making.

I think the greatest lesson I learned that summer from Willard the Wise, my granddaddy, the carpenter, was the lesson of kindness. It's demonstrated when you pass along the skills of something you hold precious to someone else.

Like a dad teaching a quiet lesson about turning a tractor, or a wise granddaddy teaching his Sonny Boy how to drive a nail. Or a Father passing along His love to and through His Son. Or that same Father teaching His adult sons how to instruct their young sons and daughters.

Three years ago I helped my son, Clarkie, drill his first hole in a piece of lumber. He was six then. Now he's nine, and we've built several little things together, nothing spectacular, but meaningful.

I'm looking forward to teaching him a few things about carpentry, and about life. Who knows? I just might start calling him "Sonny Boy." I'll definitely teach him about his heavenly Father, the One who passed along everything He knew to His Son, and then to us.

Oh yeah. I bought the motorcycle. A little Honda 70. Not very fast, but boy was it beautiful to me! Rode it up and down those little hills near my grandfather's property. I had earned almost enough to buy it brand-spanking-new—all but fourteen dollars, which I paid off two weeks later after mowing lawns in Phoenix.

The motorcycle was okay, but I'll never forget the lessons in kindness I learned with my granddaddy. I think he showed me an important part of the Father's heart, something far more important than a little motorcycle.

He showed me the ingredient that, when mixed with a teachable moment, helps the lesson stick like mud to a tractor tire. It's the ingredient called kindness.

CHAPTER SIX

At the Heart of Every Great Father
You'll Find Patience

Murle ducked his head a bit and fiddled with his ever-present white handkerchief as he responded to the pastor's request. The proposition now on the table wasn't at all what the sixty-five-year-old retiree had in mind.

"Yeah, I know I told you I'd help anywhere I could," Murle admitted, but..." He left the sentence unfinished, flapping his arms in consternation, unaware that he was waving the hanky like a flag of surrender.

"Pastor, I brought up a couple of *girls* —grownups now. I'm not sure I'd know what to do with a bunch of these little fellers."

His eyes had that trapped-animal look. He was obviously searching for a way out of the cage in which he suddenly found himself.

Pastor Jim, however, wasn't about to let his friend off the hook. "All you have to do," he said, "is treat those boys like you were treated by your dad when he took *you* fishing. C'mon, Murle. What'dya say?"

"There's not enough room in my boat for very many."

Murle wiped his forehead, casting this one last excuse as bait, hoping the pastor would bite.

No sale.

"Just take 'em two at a time," Jim said without hesitation.

"Dang it, you've thought of everything, haven't you?" Murle chuckled in spite of himself.

"Well? Will you do it?"

"Oh shoot, Pastor, I *suppose* so—for what good it might do." And then he threw in, "All except that Sammy kid." Murle felt sure the pastor would understand about him.

Jim flashed a knowing grin. He knew about Sammy.

"You just start taking them two by two, and we'll pray about little Sammy," said the younger man with a twinkle in his eye.

Murle made good on his promise. He began taking the boys out, two at a time. Many of the young fishermen had very little dad influence in their homes. Murle provided a touch of manhood in the lads' lives.

Six weeks after he began filling his Saturdays with bluegill, bass, and boys, Murle stood in the church office, nervously swiping the beads of perspiration on his forehead as he spoke to the pastor. "He just came runnin' up after church this morning."

"Who did, Murle?" asked Jim, watching the hanky dab at the old gent's shiny head.

"That Sammy kid! He said the other boys had all got a chance and could he please have a chance, too?" Up went the handkerchief.

Pastor Jim raised an eyebrow and smiled. "Oh, the fishing trips. And Sammy wants to go, too, huh? Well...what do you think?"

Down went the hanky, crumpled into a ball. Murle shook his head. "I dunno, Pastor. You know this one. He's enough trouble by himself to sink two boats!"

"You pray about it and then do what you think best, Murle." Jim smiled as he gave his friend a couple of solid pats on the shoulder. He turned to walk away.

"Pastor!" Murle called, stuffing the hanky in his back pocket.

"Yes?" Jim stopped in the doorway.

"Okay. *Okay*, I'll take him...but by himself. With him, one's enough!"

"Good, Murle. Good."

Saturday morning a screech of tires sent Jim bolt upright in his chair at the church office.

He left his sermon notes and was headed toward the parking lot when Murle burst through the door at the end of the long hallway, huffing and puffing. All the way down the hall, he kept muttering, "He did it. He *did* it!"

"Who did what, Murle?" Jim knew his friend was flustered because he'd left his pickup truck so fast he had forgotten his handkerchief.

"Little Sammy. He DID it. I can't believe it." The old man was pacing back and forth, rubbing his hands up and down the sides of his jeans.

"Murle, take a couple of nitros and calm down. What did he do? You haven't even gotten out of the parking lot yet."

"I know, I *know*. The little minnow just blurted out and asked me *how does a kid get saved*? You know—as in eternal life!"

"And...what did you say?"

"Well, I told him you have to tell Jesus you're a good-for-nothin' sinner and ask forgiveness for your sins and ask Jesus to come into your life and be the Boss."

"That's fine, Murle. You told him the right thing. But I don't understand—why did you slam on the brakes?"

"Well, the little rug rat got right down on his knees on the floorboard of my truck and started confessin' every bad thing he's ever done since he can remember! He's still at it out there!" Murle waved his hand vaguely toward the parking lot.

Pastor Jim laughed as he walked Murle out to the parking lot, where, together, they knelt with little Sammy and gave thanks to God that he had found a family. The little lad without much dad influence had just become the Father's child. And all because Murle gave a sacrificial gift of time to a young boy.

Little Sammy grew up to become a sportswriter for a prominent Florida newspaper. Years after his parking-lot confession, Sammy wrote a special column for the paper's Father's Day issue.

It was a tribute to a man named Murle.

Later still, after many such fishing trips, Murle entered eternity. At his memorial service, Sammy, now grown and with kids of his own, stood behind a pulpit and read a tribute to his friend.

It was the article he had written years earlier for a certain Father's Day. The title? "Change a little boy's life. Take him fishing."

Murle's life demonstrated that patience has its rewards.

My father demonstrated that same sacrificial gift of patience when he waited for just the right moment to spring the idea of working all summer with my grandfather so I could earn that motorcycle.

He knew that patience would be born in my life as I watched my dream unfold...one hammered nail at a time. And he knew that the true value of those carpenter's lessons would multiply as I got older and learned to appreciate the miracle of that summer.

He was right. A little patience went a long way, as you saw from the last chapter.

Even though I wanted that motorcycle so badly I could almost smell the exhaust, my dad knew I needed to develop patience. So, in order to teach *me* patience, *he* exercised patience. He knew that his kids couldn't catch it if he hadn't caught it himself.

You know what? That summer of my fourteenth year is one of the most memorable in my life. I learned about carpentry and, more importantly, about the carpenter. I also learned about hard work, and at the end of summer I had a brand-new motorcycle to show for it.

Like Murle, I learned that patience has its rewards.

And when I discovered how much that summer had meant to my grandfather, I realized that those who *give* the gift of patience earn rewards of their own. As with Murle's story, my grandfather found a boatload of blessing by spending time with a young boy.

Later that same year my father bought himself a little dirt bike, too, so we could explore desert trails together. We ate each other's dust, crashed a couple of times in that talcum-fine stuff, and feasted on dusty sandwiches and warm lemonade from a thermos. He patiently invested himself in a kid with high-octane energy. And I'll remember those dusty trail rides *forever*.

It wasn't easy for my dad to give up his Saturdays. He could easily have painted the carport, seeded the lawn, or worked a little extra on Sunday's sermon. But instead, he turned his calendar upside down, shook out a few projects, gave a sacrificial gift of patience, and poured a little of his life into mine.

Desert dirt biking may not have been his first choice for recreation, but it was *mine*, and he wanted to be with me, doing what I enjoyed most. Now that I'm a dad, I sometimes find it hard to sit and listen to my youngest daughter babble on about Barbie dolls. I find it even more difficult to play a video game with my son, mostly because he always wins. I just about get a hook into the lip of that crafty little character trait, and it takes out some more line.

But I'm learning that the rewards for practiced patience come in many forms: the gift of a hat, a mug that says "In Dad We Trust," an unexpected hug after a backyard campout. I wouldn't trade those rewards for anything. A little seed of patience bears really sweet fruit—fruit that takes years to grow.

I don't want my kids to wriggle away from home like fish out of water simply because I didn't learn the fatherly art of patience. I'm trying to give to my kids the same gift of patience my dad gave me and Murle gave to the little kid who wouldn't sit still and Jesus still gives to guys like us.

I don't always succeed, by the way. I sometimes lose my cool and rock the boat, but when I sit still and listen to the Spirit, He shows me how to hang on. To be more accurate, He shows me that I need to *let go* and let Him hold on for me.

Boiling down Murle's experience, and my dad's, into a concentrated, personal definition of patience, here's what I get:

Helping a kid do in four hours
what you could have done yourself in thirty minutes.

And here's another way to say it:

Greater love hath no man than to give up his
golf game to take a kid fishing.

Paul the apostle—one of the greatest fishers of men who ever lived—knew that. Patience, according to him, reveals a lot more than the ability to teach a kid to fish.

In Paul's mind, patience is an audiovisual demonstration of God Himself to these adult-hungry youngsters. Paul said, "We have proved ourselves to be what we claim [God's children] by our wholesome lives and by our understanding of the Gospel and by our patience" (2 Corinthians 6:6a, TLB).

Patience given to our kids as a Spirit-motivated gift reveals the Father who is busy at work in the heart of the giver.

And, as Murle and Paul both discovered, the only way to get hold of the slippery little rascal is to give up trying to grab it by yourself and to let the Holy Spirit catch it for you. Paul said the way he obtained patience was by letting the Spirit become active in his life. "We have been kind and truly loving and filled with the Holy Spirit" (6:6b, TLB).

It's that patience-producing Spirit at work in your heart that keeps you from capsizing the boat when the waves of anger and frustration froth up white water all around.

That's what Richard Keene discovered the night his fourteen-year-old daughter, Amanda, tearfully confessed, "Dad, I'm pregnant! What am I going to do?"

Rich is a manly member of our church. The guy builds houses and does roofing and siding. He's tough. Yet that tough guy ran up against something that tested his patience more than anything he'd ever encountered.

His story could be called "Praying for Paytience." No, that's not a misprint. Paytience is spelled correctly. You'll see why in a minute.

Rich told us about his daughter's plight at our men's group meeting. We were in the middle of studying Stu Weber's book *Tender Warrior* when Rich told us about the horrible night he and his wife, Lisa, confirmed what they had suspected about their daughter—but were afraid to admit to themselves.

"We both saw the changes right before our eyes," he told us, "but we just didn't want to believe this could actually be happening to our Amanda." Rich was taking a risk by telling all this to the other guys. But he was learning that he needed our support.

He got gut-level honest with us about his angry first reactions to the news, about the questions, the raised voices, the accusations. Then he told us, "Although I was furious on the outside, inside I knew I had to accept this kid of mine who was going to have a kid of her own. So I forced myself to do something I guess I knew deep down would be the right thing. I walked over to her, held out my arms, and hugged her.

"She was really fighting her feelings, 'cause she didn't know how to act. At first she was stiff and didn't really hug me back.

"Then I said, 'Amanda, we're going to get through this...together. What you did was wrong—but that's my grandchild in there.'"

That was a turning point for the entire family. Rich continued, "I didn't know how I would react to something like this—it was like a badly scripted TV show—but without thinking, I patted her tummy and said, 'We've got to get this baby into the world.'"

Rich's words tore into each of us guys. We didn't know how to react, but all around the room guys started telling Rich, "You did the right thing, buddy," and "Good job, man."

Fortunately Amanda didn't have to think twice about abortion. She knew that with Jesus, nothing is wasted. That baby may have been a surprise to her and her parents, but it was no surprise to God.

But she did wonder whether she was capable of providing for her child. So she poured out her doubts and tears to her parents and to my wife, Joy. Richard and Lisa told us that they would support Amanda in either of the two decisions she was considering, keeping the baby or putting it up for adoption.

Rich had told her, "Amanda, you pray about it and let us know what you decide. We'll support you either way." That's not what he told our men's group, though. He told the guys, "I really hope she keeps the baby. I mean, after all, it *is* my grandchild."

Through the two agonizing weeks that followed Richard's painful admission, we all prayed for him and Lisa—and for Amanda and the baby, too. All that time Rich was thinking, "I know I signed on for this parenting stuff, but good grief..." He told us frankly that he had really been fighting the urge to do something stupid, like leave the family or tell Amanda she had to leave. He said, "I didn't think about that stuff for very long, but I have to admit those thoughts crossed my mind. I really need an extra dose of patience right now, guys."

This lengthy ordeal was patience under construction for Rich, Lisa, Amanda, and many of us who were praying for them all. We knew God could provide, but knowing it and acting on it are two different things.

Amanda's actions affected many other people in our church and our family, including our oldest daughter, Katheryn, who was nine at the time. She reacted with shock and anger to the news that Amanda was expecting. Amanda was our children's baby-sitter, and Katheryn was especially fond of her.

Katheryn angrily poured out her heart to her mother, "She *lied* to me."

Joy asked, "What do you mean?"

"When she would baby-sit us, she would see these commercials on TV, showing young girls who had gotten pregnant, and she'd tell us, 'That's right. You should wait until you're married to have kids.' And now *she's* going to have a baby."

Katheryn didn't know what to do with all her confusing emotions, so she went to her room and cried. She stayed angry with Amanda for two solid weeks.

Meanwhile Rich kept coming to our men's group meetings, and we kept praying. He told us one night, "I can't believe how it's happening, but God seems to be giving me the ability to love Amanda when I feel like blowing up at her. I know it can't be me that's doing that, so I'd like to thank you for your prayers. They seem to be working. God's giving me patience where I didn't have any before."

About two weeks after that meeting something happened that was as unexpected as Sammy's parking-lot confession.

Weeks before Rich's painful discovery about his future grandbaby, I had already prepared a message on forgiveness. We had all been praying for the family, and I knew many people would be thinking of Amanda through the sermon. Wrestling with my conscience, I almost changed the topic the night before, thinking the church might figure I'd preached it especially for her. But I decided to go ahead with the message as planned.

At the end of the service we all stood to sing about "grace that is greater than all our sins." Halfway through the first verse, my voice cracked, and I had to stop singing.

People in the congregation looked around, trying to spot the reason for my distraction.

Walking toward me up the aisle were Amanda and her parents, Richard and Lisa. All three were crying. When they got to the front, I asked them if they wanted to ask for prayer. Amanda was weeping so hard I could barely understand her, but in between huge sobs, she choked out, "I would like...to ask forgiveness...from the church because...what I did was wrong. But I also want...to ask...for their prayers, because...I decided to...keep the baby."

With her parents beside her, Amanda bravely stood before a crowd of people who very easily could have judged her. But thanks to her parents' patience and support, she faced the crowd and admitted what she had done was wrong.

Amanda was weeping so hard by then that I had to finish bringing her request to the church. I said, "Amanda has also told me that she knows two wrongs don't make a right. It was wrong for her to get pregnant before she married, but she has made it clear that she does not want to abort the baby. Amanda is asking for your support since she has decided to keep the baby."

I knew at that moment she had won the hearts of the congregation. You could see it in their misty eyes. So I continued, "Amanda's parents are standing here in support of her. If you will support not only Amanda and this precious baby but also Richard and Lisa, would you stand, too?"

Instantly the whole congregation was on its feet. Together, Richard, Lisa, and Amanda knelt at the front of our church.

After I found my voice, I prayed, "Thank You, Father, God of comfort, and giver of life. We come, first asking forgiveness for Amanda, who admits openly she has sinned by not staying inside Your boundary, the boundary of marriage.

"And we come thanking You for Your forgiveness and grace. We thank You, Father, that a precious baby—one who won't become a wasted leftover—has found a family. Help us to act as graciously and with as much forgiveness toward Amanda and her family as You do toward us. In the name of

Jesus, Your precious Son, I pray. Amen."

As everyone filed by after that prayer, affirming their support to Amanda, I saw my daughter Katheryn dart quickly out the side door. I was afraid she was still upset. In a few minutes, though, she reappeared at the end of the line of people still giving hugs and encouragement.

She held something behind her back. I moved a couple of feet to my left so I could see Katheryn. I watched as she handed her baby-sitter a freshly handpicked bouquet of flowers from behind the church. The pianist played softly, "Grace is Greater Than Our Sins."

At the time this is being written, Amanda is seventeen years old. She still lives with her parents and is finishing high school at a special learning center where young moms bring their babies to be cared for as they study. She works part-time to earn money for diapers and clothes for the baby, and she still baby-sits for several church members, bringing her baby with her when she does. The congregation has fallen in love with the little darling. And all three of my kids, including Katheryn, adore the baby.

It hasn't been at all easy for Amanda or her parents, and they have struggled with mountains of bills to pay and valleys of emotions to conquer, but they are making it. They have a lot of support.

Amanda was only fourteen when she got pregnant and fifteen when she gave birth to that beautiful little girl. The baby's name?

Paytience.

That's why we really mean it when we say, "Pray for Paytience."

We still do. And we still pray for patience for Richard and Lisa. They have a big family, and the wire of stress gets strung pretty tight. But as we are discovering, long-term, commitment-based, Spirit-led patience has its rewards.

The sacrificial gift of patience touches a lot of people, whether it's time given to a lad with no dad, a teenager obsessed with dirt bikes, or a little girl in need of a family.

That's one character quality we can't afford to throw back in the lake.

Patience—and Paytience—are both keepers. And both are very near the heart of the Father.

CHAPTER SEVEN

At the Heart of Every Great Father
You'll Find Peace

It was a day that contained some good news, some bad news, and some really bad news.

The good news is: We planted a tree.

It was "Earth Day," and the kids brought home a baby Michigan white pine. So with a tip of the hat to political correctness as defined by the Michigan public school system, we fetched a shovel to plant it.

The bad news is: We fertilized my daughter's new white pine...with "Spot," her beloved pet goldfish.

The *really* bad news is: I killed Spot.

There's no denying it; I cooked Spot's hash. But I didn't mean to. Really. This wasn't an act of premeditated flushing. I simply didn't think to check the temperature of the water before running it into the plastic bag.

Okay, I know this is sounding pretty pathetic, but let me explain.

I was cleaning out the fishbowl, something I had never attempted in my life as a dad. I thought it made perfectly good sense to plunk the little critter into a bag of water, where he would stay until his little home wasn't so cloudy, and then I would simply dump him back in, water and all, where he would swim around, happily singing, "I can see clearly now, the crud is gone…"

After all, he had come home in a little travel-trailer baggie, so why not treat him to a campout in one? He was probably bored with the same circular scenery all day: rocks, plants, plastic ship, rocks, plants, plastic ship, rocks, plants…

Unfortunately I hadn't actually *filled* the plastic bag with water *before* I put in the fish. This may seem like a major over-sight on my part, but it was an easy mistake considering that I was preoccupied with other important matters, like the thinning ozone layer, ground-water pollution, the imminent destruction of the planet, and other sobering facts my kids had been dumping on me like toxic waste ever since they had rushed in after school.

It was a shock to my system when I plopped the little fellow into the bag only to discover that he flopped around in there like, well, a fish out of water. Evidently my system wasn't the only one shocked by this unfortunate turn of events. Old Spot's eyes suddenly appeared even more bulgy than normal.

In order to compensate for his rather immediate need for water, I did what any resourceful, quick-thinking dad would do. I reached over, stuck the baggie under the sink faucet and cranked on the handle for the cold water. This probably would have solved Spot's problem, except…

Do you know what happens when you turn on the cold water after your wife has been running the hot water for the dishes? In our house the hot water stays inside the faucet for a few minutes. So, technically speaking, although I officially turned the handle marked "C," I unofficially doused the poor, unsuspecting, little goldfish with what Spot would have considered *really* hot water.

I don't know for sure whether it was the lack of water at first, the shock of leaving his secure surroundings, the sudden jolt of a bumpy ride in his little travel baggie, or the almost boiling water that did poor Spot in. Maybe it was a combination of these factors. But at any rate, Spot rather quickly ceased being part of our family that afternoon. And, as strange as it may seem, we all started learning lessons about the real meaning of the word *peace*.

It wasn't as though this was the first Cothern family pet to cash it in. We had weathered a couple of traumatic, teachable-moment death experiences before. There was Fluffy Grayson, the cutest hamster this side of the pet store. And of course there was Snuffles the bunny, who didn't quite survive the sensational scorching summer of '93. But for some inexplicable reason, the loss of our fish, Spot, in his little watery grave revealed a tidal wave of emotions far greater than any of us were aware.

Our kids dealt with the news of Spot's demise in their individual ways. Callie's lower lip turned inside out, and she walked to her room where she cried for about ten minutes. Clarkie's mood turned somber, but he toughed it out and stubbornly resisted the urge to stop playing kickball in the backyard.

Katheryn, our oldest, was very sad but seemed more concerned about consoling her younger sister, Callie (first child, you know).

We survived the ordeal that day and had a meaningful "funeral" for Spot out by the new little Michigan white pine, where they each said a few kind words over their departed friend:

—"He was a very good swimmer."

—"He used to look at me with his mouth doing that fish thing, and he made me laugh."

—"He never argued."

Then I took off for a meeting while the kids got busy playing again.

Ah, it seemed at the time that peace had once again been restored to the Cothern household. Later that evening, however, when I arrived home, I walked into the girls' room just in time to both ignite and observe a volcanic eruption of unseen feelings. Joy was comforting the kids when this conversation rumbled forth:

Callie: "Oh, hi, Daddy. Dad? I still love you (muffled sobs), but...I'm willy, willy sad (bigger sobs)...'cause you put the fishy in the baggie and put in the willy, willy hot water... (*sniffle*, willy big sobs)...and you *killed* Spot! (Wahhhh!)"

Daddy: "I know, Callie. I feel so bad about that. I didn't know the water would come out so hot." (Lesson: Excuses don't work at times like these. Just plain "Sorry" is best.)

Katie: "Daddy?"

Daddy: "Yes, honey?"

Katie: (sigh) "I know you didn't *mean* to kill Spot (*sniffle*). I know it was an accident."

Daddy: "Thank you, Katie. I'm really sorry about it, though." (I was glad she understood.)

Katie: "Daddy?"

Daddy: "Yes, honey?"

Katie: "Can I stay home from school tomorrow so we can go pick out another fish?"

Daddy: "No, honey." (Katie was beginning to accept her loss.)

Katie: "Okay."

The surprise came when Clarkie weighed into the conversation.

Clarkie: "At least now Nancy Sibley has a pet fish up in heaven (*sniffle*), but now...(*bigger sniffle*)...*I miss Nancy Sibley.*" With that, my son started to sob.

That's when the heat from the pain lying deep and dormant burst forth into full flame. For all of us. Our young friend Nancy Sibley had died a few months before.

Nancy was not a casual acquaintance. She had been born on the exact same day as our son. Our family was the first to know about Nancy, because her parents had secretly told us they were going to adopt her.

We had welcomed Nancy to her new home, had watched her grow up in the church nursery, and had grown to love her as a special friend. Jokes had even been made about our son and Nancy having an "arranged" marriage. "After all," friends would say, "they're perfect for each other. And they were born on the same day. It's a sign."

Of course we laughed at these comments, but because of the similarities we shared with the family, we had grown very attached.

So it was, as you can imagine, a thunderous shock when we got the phone call from a friend: "Nancy Sibley has had a terrible accident. She's at Mott's Children's Hospital in Ann Arbor."

And the caller paused to gather her thoughts and keep herself from crying so hard we wouldn't be able to understand her.

"We—we don't know if she will survive."

You know that sound you make when you don't know what to say? As if someone has just punched you as hard as he can right in the gut? That's the sound I made. I couldn't help asking some of the inevitable questions. "How did it happen? Why wasn't an adult nearby? Why didn't...?"

At that moment none of those questions really mattered. But I felt compelled to ask them anyway, if for no other reason than to try to make some sense of this senseless tragedy.

The distraught caller provided a few of the answers. "Her parka drawstring got hung on a school slide. A child ran to get an adult, but by the time they got back, Nancy was already unconscious. They think she was without oxygen for several minutes."

At first I couldn't find my breath. It was hard work just to utter, "Okay, thanks."

As quickly as I could get my mind working, I told Joy what I had just been told, and she arranged for someone in our church to watch our kids. We drove to the hospital, where we waited and prayed, paced and prayed, and sat in silence and prayed with the hundred other friends who had gathered for support.

Then the hospital chaplain finally walked in with "that look"—that drawn-tight-around-the-eyes, grief-stricken look. (Chaplains, God bless them, have difficult jobs to do.) He sighed deeply, shook his head slightly, and said, "The tests came back with the news we've all dreaded. The doctors don't find any brain activity. I'm sorry."

Have you ever heard an entire room filled with people suddenly go completely silent? I heard it that afternoon. No one was even breathing. We all just sat, staring, for about ten seconds, until someone remembered to thank the chaplain for his part in this strange event, and he began explaining that we were all invited to say our good-byes.

The kind of silence I heard that afternoon was not peace. Lack of noise does not equal peace. Yet we were all digging deeper, about to come face to face with the real definition.

In little groups of two or three we walked softly into the stark little room, where silence hung heavy over the machinery that had previously been beeping and humming.

Lovingly, gently, dear friends gingerly touched Nancy's pale skin, as pale as it had ever been, since she was strongly and darkly influenced by her Korean birth mother. They hugged the only mother Nancy had known—her adoptive mother—as she sat, bravely facing the most painful day of her brief motherhood. A little over five years. Not at all long enough to retire from the job.

When it was my turn to enter, I stood in the doorway and took a mental snapshot of Ron, our deacon friend, bent over little Nancy, softly stroking her thick, black hair.

I thought I heard singing.

But then I thought, *Nah. Ron wouldn't be singing.* For one thing he has a deep, bass voice, and for another thing his deep bass voice is usually booming and powerful.

Ron had nicknamed Nancy "Tigger" because she bounced everywhere she went. She wasn't bouncy now. She was lying so still it made you want to shake her, to say, "Nancy, come on, wake up. Move!"

I was sure I heard something, though, that sounded like singing. It sounded like when you turn the treble all the way down on your car radio and play the classical station really low. More of a rumble, actually, than music.

Yes, I was sure I heard it, but I couldn't quite make out what was being sung, so I edged just a bit closer.

Up to this point I had fought back the tears. I remember thinking, *Why do they use the word "brave" for those who don't cry?*

As I came within hearing range of my manly friend Ron, I decided that bravery had nothing to do with holding back tears. He was one of the bravest men I had met, and yet tears were streaming down his face.

In his deep, rumbly voice, Ron was singing, ever so softly, "Jesus loves me, this I know. For the Bible tells me so. Little ones to Him belong. They are weak but He is strong."

"Oh, man," I whispered. And then again, *"Oh, man."* And I decided to quit fighting and just let go and cry. Shoot. Why not? Everyone else was.

Trust me on this one, you don't quickly forget scenes like that.

It was an afternoon when all the "why" questions were left dangling, along with the wires hanging from those awful, silent machines. No, this crushing silence was not peace. How does a parent find peace in an emergency room when the machines stop beeping?

Our kids went to Nancy's funeral. We wanted them to. They needed to know about life and death and eternity. And peace.

They cried. We cried. They watched a lot of other people cry. They looked at Nancy's little body in the casket. They listened as adults talked about a God who loves kids, about a God who doesn't cause bad things to happen to five-year-olds.

And then they scooted up to the edge of their seats and listened very closely to a dear friend—the manly singing deacon—as he spoke.

"Nancy accomplished more in her five act—"

He stopped. Five act what? A five-act play?

He swallowed and tried again. "In her five active years—"

Oh, that was it. Ron had choked up. I silently prayed, *Lord, give him strength to get through this.*

"...in her five years of life than most of us will accomplish in eighty-five years."

He was gaining strength. He took one more deep breath and continued, stronger and more boldly.

"Nancy told everybody she met that she loved Jesus."

I had rarely seen my kids so attentive in church before. They were hanging on every word.

"If you could draw a time line that starts right here on the floor of this building," he said, pointing, "and extend that line up through the ceiling and on up through space, past the farthest star, and continue that line as far as it could go, and then some, off into eternity..."

My kids were following Ron's motions. They were seeing that invisible line.

"...then five years marked on that line would be like this!" He snapped his fingers. We all began to get his point. "But if you could mark off eighty-five years on that time line, it, too, would seem like this." And he snapped them again.

"Nancy did the most important thing any of us could ever do. She took care of the real business of this life. She made peace with her Creator. She accepted Jesus Christ into her heart and life. She knew Jesus as a Friend. Nancy is with her Friend. She's at peace."

That was it. That's the real meaning of the peculiar peace that can rest down deep, so far we don't even know it's there until...something like this happens. Peace that doesn't make any earthly sense. Peace that outweighs a roomful of silent machines. Peace that goes way beyond human understanding. Peace that has a *name*. It's spelled J-E-S-U-S.

Ron finished his words of strength and comfort—and peace—and we all steadied ourselves for the next item on this incredible program.

We sat, amazed that Nancy's mom would even attempt what she did. She read a couple of significant pages from Nancy's favorite book. It was Max Lucado's book *In Case You've Ever Wondered*.

She got through the book without losing it, even though the rest of us were basket cases. We heard that, in case we ever wondered, those of us who know Jesus would never have to be alone, or in the dark, or scared, or in pain when we get to heaven, because Jesus made it possible for us to be with Him. And He loves us *very* much, just in case we ever wondered.

Then we heard people talking about how good it's going to be when they see their friend Nancy again. We saw people who were calm in the depths of their souls, even though the storm was welling up on the surface.

And then all of us—and millions more through television coverage—watched an incredible display of strength and

Spirit-motivated peace, as Nancy's mother, Thelma Sibley, refused to blame others for the accident that killed her only daughter.

Thelma and her husband, Bob, are wonderful examples of grace under pressure, since they publicly stated, "Nancy's death was no one's fault. Everyone did everything they could under the circumstances. It was just a terrible accident. We just want to keep this from happening to someone else's little girl or boy."

Nancy's death lit a fire under Thelma's already-strong resolve to make the world a better place. Thelma allowed the Holy Spirit to transform her negative feelings of grief into posi-tive action to save other children from such a horrible accident. She spoke with confidence and with Spirit-filled peace to committees in Washington, D.C., to presidents of clothing companies, and on talk shows all across the country, successfully persuading garment manufacturers all over America to alter their clothing designs to produce children's coats without drawstrings.

Whew. What courage. What peace.

Because I'm a minister, my wife and I see a lot of grieving people. We know grief takes time. We know little things can trigger a grief response. But, like the plumber whose sink at home is stopped up, we ministers sometimes fail to notice when our own painful emotions are plugged up.

So we were a bit surprised when Spot's death stirred up intense feelings still swimming around inside all of us.

We didn't even connect Spot with Nancy until the kids did.

But all it took was one brief comment from our son, and we all started remembering.

That was where *I* almost lost it. My tough little son's tender remark about his friend Nancy caught me as off guard as the hot water pouring into Spot's baggie. It reminded me that death—and eternal life—were still very much on their minds. And now, thanks to my kids, these important matters were on mine, too.

Three precious children innocently poured out their hearts as two stunned parents listened, held them close, and tried to make sense of this surprise lesson in grief adjustment.

Callie, who was then only three, reminded us that we will have new bodies in heaven. And, in her mind, so will a goldfish named Spot. (Baggies in heaven all have cold water, by the way. I have it on good authority.)

Clarkie, then six, caused us to imagine kids playing and growing in heaven. I couldn't see anything wrong with that notion. And I still don't find any scripture that says we'll just loaf around on a cloud all day plucking a harp. It's helpful to realize our eternal future will be exciting and full of new opportunities. It just takes a child's eye to visualize it.

Katie, then eight years old, reminded us that bad accidents happen to good people. She reminded me that I ought to trust God instead of blaming Him when things go wrong, knowing that He wants the very best for us. He can still hold things together even when we're falling apart.

Thanks to these mature reminders from young children, we began to experience peace in the middle of our crisis. It's the kind of peace that calms the depths even though the storm still rages on the surface.

I knew God brought good out of bad, but up to that point

it had been hard to accept the "good" that came out of Nancy's death. My children helped me see that God can turn even a tragedy like Nancy's accident into something good. They helped me picture that vivacious little girl enjoying an abundant, eternal life with her heavenly Father—a Father who loves her more than we ever possibly could.

And they helped me find peace.

But that kind of peace takes time. When the ceiling is falling in on your life, you don't just snap your fingers and whip up a batch of peace. Even the strongest believers have asked the why questions.

In fact, if you listen closely, you can hear the words, "If you had only been here..." as they echo down through the corridors of time, through the hospital halls, into the ICU room where a set of bewildered parents struggle to cling to their composure as they hold onto a lifeless little girl.

The words had been spoken by strong, upstanding, God-fearing, Jesus-loving people. Martha and Mary. Ladies who had helped Jesus on His journeys. Good friends of the Teacher who had hosted Him in their home many times. They knew Him more personally than most of us can imagine, yet when their brother died, they felt alone. And they struggled to find someone to blame for their feelings. So they blamed Jesus.

"If you had only been here," they said. First Martha, then Mary. Two separate accounts, spoken at two different times, yet the words were almost identical. *"If you had only been here."* They speak for most of us, don't they? Isn't that how we feel sometimes?

I've met people just like Martha and Mary. People who act in church as though God is on His throne and all is right with the world. But secretly, at home, in the quiet loneliness of the dark hours after a tragedy, standing in an empty room, looking at a closet filled with clothes—clothes that still smell like... Then those people become just as human as the rest of us.

And they shout at heaven, "If You had only been here. Where *were* You, God?"

People like the waitress who opened up to some friends of mine.

When Bruce and his wife, Cindy, told her what a good job she had done, she responded by saying, "Thanks for the compliment. I needed it. It's been a hard year."

They looked at each other then back at her. "Year?"

"Yeah. I lost my father, my husband, and one of my children."

"All in one year?"

"Yeah. It's been tough."

Bruce, normally very talkative, was at a complete loss for words. What can you say at a time like that? Cindy tried to give her a bit of assurance, but even the typical, "I'm sorry. I know it must have been hard, but have faith," kind of lines come out sounding as hollow as the hospital halls in ICU.

Bruce finally reached for some word of encouragement: "I know it doesn't feel like it right now, but God really does love you, even when you're hurting."

Her flat answer left him in one of those semidepressed, introspective moods. She said, "Yeah? Well, He sure has a funny way of showin' it."

That's what our friends Bob and Thelma Sibley felt at times. "I know God loves us, but right now it seems like He sure has a funny way of showing it."

Jesus had told Martha and Mary all about His plans for their eternal future, and they were thrilled about it. They felt strong and hopeful when they were in His presence. But when they were choking for the breath that was taken away from them by Lazarus's death—a death that could have been prevented if Jesus had only been there—they felt like we all do in times like that. Lonely. Abandoned. Forsaken. Angry. Empty. Sad. Confused.

It was get-to-the-point Martha, the more outspoken of the two sisters, who hurried to meet Jesus even before He got into town. She looked Him right in the eyes and told Him things we wish we could say but usually don't. She said, "If You had only been here, our brother wouldn't have died!"

I have a friend who, in his tongue-in-cheek way, would tell her, "Don't hold back, Martha. Tell Him how you *really* feel."

She didn't hold back. And there's the strange part of the story. Wouldn't you expect the Lord of Lords and King of Kings to push her aside, point an authoritative finger, and say, "How *dare* you speak to Me like that! Do you realize who you're talking to?"

But Jesus didn't do that. He was very purposeful in His actions. Lazarus's death didn't take Jesus by surprise. Nothing did. In fact, Jesus had waited on purpose—on *purpose*—until *after* His close friend Lazarus had expired before traveling to town to see him. He had said so Himself.

Do you think some of Jesus' close friends gossiped to Martha and Mary about His intention to wait? I don't know. If they found out He had waited on purpose, I can see why Martha would be ticked off.

I can just imagine her, in an animated, hyperemotional state, saying, "You mean to tell me You *knew* my brother was dying, and You just *sat* there? What were You thinking? Certainly not of us, were You? If You had only thought of *us*, You'd know how badly we're hurting right now. You probably can't imagine the pain. Well, I hope You're satisfied. He's gone. Our brother is *gone*. And You did nothing, *nothing* to stop his death!"

That's not what was actually recorded in Scripture, though. I'm not sure Martha said those words. I'm fairly certain, since I'm a human being and have been around other grieving human beings, that she must have at least *thought* words like those. Haven't we all?

And that's why I'm totally blown away by Jesus' response to Martha. He didn't condemn her. He didn't preach at her for her snippy behavior. He offered her words of peace. He said, "Your brother will rise again." (Hear it? The peace deep down inside?)

Martha must have thought this was one of those pastoral pat answers, kept on hand for just such an occasion. "Oh yes, he's in a better place now," or "At least he's not suffering anymore."

Those things are usually true when those we've lost have been believers, but they seem as empty as Bruce's comment to the waitress who had lost three loved ones in twelve months.

At least Martha was faithful enough to recognize the promise of life after death. She said, "I know he will rise again in the resurrection at the last day." I don't know how she said those words, but I humanly want to write in the word "however..." after her sentence. Maybe her face said it. I want to superimpose my feelings over her phrase and add to it, "But what about the empty feeling I have right now? What about this turmoil, this earthquake in my soul that has left me reeling and grasping for something to steady my balance?"

Jesus had to have known all those feelings. He was human, too. And without skipping a beat, He added more fuel to the fire of faith He had started to kindle in this grieving friend.

He said, "I am the resurrection and the life. He who believes in me will live, even though he dies; and whoever lives and believes in me will never die. Do you believe this?" (John 11:25–26). (There it is again. That low, deep, bass rumble of peace.)

And as she looked at the One who had just claimed that *He* was the resurrection and the life—not someone who could help her find peace but the One who *is* peace—she found herself able to reaffirm those words we all should say over and over again when we feel lost and alone and abandoned and hurt: "I believe that you are the Christ, the Son of God" (11:27).

Martha had just found the secret to peace. She put her finger on something so incredible yet simple that it escapes most people. She spoke words that echoed all the way to that hospital room where grieving people were wrestling with the same questions and feelings.

Through tears of grief, Martha and Thelma were able to whisper—in a faith that may have started out as small as a tiny mustard seed but blossomed into a huge tree as they watered it with their tears—"You are the Christ."

His presence was enough. That's where they found peace.

Hear it? Echoing down the halls of time into the emergency

room? There it is again, louder this time. And it spills out in the low, deep, bass, rumbly voice of Ron the deacon. "Jesus loves me, this I know, for the Bible tells me so..."

Then, just like our children's emotional flashback that pushed up to the surface all those buried feelings, the whole scene was repeated before Jesus as Mary followed in her sister's footsteps. Grief, I suppose, requires many such episodes, until the waves become smaller and the time between them greater.

This time, with Mary, a new element is added to Jesus' words—actions. Actions that showed just how much Christ really cared, even though His friends may have thought otherwise.

Just as Martha was absorbing the impact of Jesus' healing words, Mary came along and blurted out the exact phrase Martha had unloaded moments earlier, "If you had been here, my brother would not have died."

Jesus had kept his composure with Martha. He was steady-voiced and solid as a rock. (And why not? He *is* the Rock.) And then He saw Mary. It's not hard to stay strong for one crying friend, but when a second starts blubbering, the emotions peg the meter.

That big, husky deacon in the hospital knew Nancy's ultimate destination. Yet when he saw the hurt etched deeply in both parents' faces, when he imagined that this could have been one of his daughters, when he suddenly felt the fist tighten in his own stomach in empathy with the knockout punch he was witnessing in two of his closest friends, he caved in.

Ron's tears were perhaps the most Christlike thing he did that day. Because, in a similar situation years earlier, Jesus looked at His friends, and though He knew the ultimate outcome of their brother, his friend, He too wept, right along with them.

If peace were the absence of tears, then people in denial—with deep rage shoved down deeper with each passing hour—would be the most "peaceful." But it doesn't work that way. Somehow, curiously, peace is often found in shared tears.

Thomas Moore said, "Earth hath no sorrow that heaven can't heal." First Martha, then her sister, Mary, and then years later, their younger sister in Christ, Thelma, understood that phrase to be true.

Each in her own way and in her own time, painstakingly swam against wave after wave of the drowning, depressing sadness and despair that threatened to hurl her overboard into an ocean so dark and deep she thought she would never survive.

And each time the wave would crash over them, they would whisper the words: "You are the Christ, the Son of God." And just as they were ready to give up the fight and sink into the ocean of their own tears, Jesus appeared to say, "I am the resurrection and the life."

And even though He *is* that peace, even though He is the One who will dry all our tears when we finally arrive in heaven, Christ looks with empathy at us when we are hurting, and He cries right along with us. Just like Ron in that emergency room.

Peace is found not in the absence of tears but in the presence of Christ.

A humble little goldfish reminded us of that fact. Funny, isn't it, what God can use to draw out the pain of our past so we can learn the peace of His presence?

Dads, you can model that same kind of peace for your children, the kind that says through the tears, "You are the Christ, the Son of God." It may not seem possible when the unexpected rogue winds whip up a rough sea around you, but if you'll just whisper those words, "You are the Christ," you'll be on the right path to peace. And your kids will see a strength in you they want in their own lives. At the heart of every great father is peace, the kind that cries through the waves and the tears, "You are the Christ."

Learn to say those words, and you won't have to weather the storms alone.

At the end of our family learning experience after Spot's untimely departure came another unexpected lesson from our youngest. Our kids re-asked questions we had all asked, like, "Didn't the other kids try to help get Nancy off that slide?"

"Yes, they did. But when they couldn't get her free, they all ran inside to get a teacher to help."

"Wasn't there a 'big person' on the playground?"

"Yes, but they were helping the other kids go inside since recess was over."

"You mean...she was all alone?"

That question, above all others, left me stunned.

I couldn't think of anything more frightening than to be all alone at such a time. I could tell my kids were thinking the same thing. But as the lump rose in my throat, closing off the words I was searching for, little Callie spoke up.

"No! Nancy *wasn't* alone!" She was firm. Bold. Assertive.

"She had two angels there with her. One was holding up her left elbow, and the other one was holding up her right elbow." She spoke with such confidence and in such detail.

Ah, the wonderful wisdom of a child. I believe little Callie was absolutely right. And why not? Angels ushered in the baby Jesus. Angels announced His birth. Angels rejoice when a sinner repents and says, "You *are* the Christ. *You* are the resurrection and the life!" Angels were present at all the most important moments of history, and angels will announce Christ's return.

So why not a pair of angels, sent to escort Nancy Sibley into her glorious, eternal, new life?

Nancy was *not* alone.

She had a pair of angels saying, "Fear not, Nancy. Be at peace. We're almost Home, little one."

Nancy was not alone. And neither were we. We held each other and cried. And in our shared tears we found peace.

All in all, I'd say it was a pretty important day in the life of a family and in the life and death of a fish named Spot, who helped us discover a peculiar peace—not peace defined as the absence of anxiety, but peace that comes from not being alone.

The Father had allowed us to glimpse what He has placed at the heart of every great father—the peace of His presence. And that kind of peace has a name.

Jesus.

CHAPTER EIGHT

At the Heart of Every Great Father
You'll Find Joy

———<small>c/c/c</small>———

A nd I thought to myself, *I'm dead meat.*"
These words were uttered at the very moment my eyes landed on the juicy slab of sirloin—still sizzling on its piping hot metal platter—that traveled past my nose and out of the server's hand onto the table in front of me.

My parents, my sister, and I all laughed as the waitress, wondering what joke she had just walked into, said, "Must have been a good one."

"Aw," I replied, "you'd have to be there."

We all took a whiff of the tantalizing food and gave thanks for God's blessings, including the fact that we were together, as one family, for the first time in several years.

I had flown from my home in Michigan to Phoenix, Arizona, to spend a week with my folks. With twenty-two hundred miles and big-bucks plane tickets separating me from my parents and my sister, Kathey, and her two boys, it was easy to let time fly by without catching up with each other.

Here we were, though, at the famous La Casa Vieja steakhouse, located across the street from the Hayden Mills in

Tempe, Arizona. Just stepping into the place made you want to walk bowlegged and reach for your chewing tobacco.

Saddles and tack decorated the entryway, and the incredible hickory grill smell that greeted you at the door said, "Yessiree, c'mon in and make yerself at home, pardner."

Between the salad and the main course, someone in our little foursome headed the conversation down the dusty trail of our growing-up years. I was smack-dab in the middle of one of those stories when the waitress brought our meals.

It was the one about when I was home alone with Dad, who was at work in his study. While he was busy trying to concentrate, I was busy playing, loudly, by batting around a balloon in the living room. He walked in from his study and shot me a .357-magnum look.

When I got to that part in my story, I portrayed my dad as the Clint Eastwood type, walking in with dusty chaps and a tattered cowboy hat. I whistled the theme from *The Outlaw Josey Wales* and faked a spit into a nearby spittoon.

That's when the waitress killed the story by stomping all over my line about my thinking I was about to become dead meat. After she left and we said our prayer, I resumed the regularly scheduled tale, still in progress.

"So *anyway*," I continued, "Dad walks in, and I'm all set to get taken to the woodshed with his speech. I thought he'd say, 'I'm trying to study. Put that thing away and find something constructive to do!' I was expecting a shootout at the OK Corral, but Dad didn't pull out his big guns and fire away.

"Instead, his narrow-eyed look quickly melted into a goofy grin, and he asked, 'Wanna play balloon volleyball?'

"I couldn't believe it. Dad tied one end of a string to a lamp and the other end to the stereo..."

Mom faked a disgusted look at Dad and interrupted, "You did *what?*" (It was a good thing Mom didn't find out about the string until several years after the event. If she had seen us abusing her living room like that, she would have exiled us both to the backyard—or to the panhandle of Texas.)

"Yeah, and we served, set, and spiked that crazy balloon around for a good half-hour until we were both rolling on the floor, exhausted and laughing."

"Do you remember that?" I asked my dad.

He wiped a tear that had crept out while laughing and said, "No. It sounds unbelievable. I can't for the life of me remember when that happened. Sounds like I had a great time, though!"

He had forgotten the famed balloon volleyball tournament, but I recalled it vividly. Why? Because to a kid, that's the stuff joy is made of. That's because...

joy = companionship

That's the formula, plain and simple. That's what we determined in our steak-eating, sidesplitting evening together as a family, looking back on years of joyful experiences.

Chuck Swindoll, in his hilariously serious book *Laugh Again*, says, "Far too many adults I know are as serious as a heart attack.... They cannot remember when they last took a chance or risked trying something new.... I ask you, where's the fun? Let's face it, you and I are getting older—it's high time we stop acting like it!"[1]

If you've spent a day at the zoo with your kids when you felt like a caged animal, fighting back roars of anger because you'd rather be home working on your latest pet project, you know what I'm talking about. Becoming a companion with your children is hard work and costs you some "personal time." But believe me, friend, it's worth it. As my sister would say, "If you don't believe me, just ask me."

After Kathey and I related a few of those zoolike experiences from our own parenting-story files, Dad admitted that when we were kids he had endured many anxious Saturday afternoons, times when he would much rather have worked on his sermon than throw the baseball with me in the backyard or listen to Kath's latest boy crisis.

At our steakhouse reunion I said to my father, "Now that I'm old enough to inherit your workaholic tendencies, I'll confess there are days when I'd love to lock my kids in the basement, put in earplugs, and get some work done!" He laughed.

"But I don't," I added, "...*most* of the time." We all laughed.

I took another bite of steak and sighed with total contentment at the good food and the great company of my family. "Just the other day," I went on, "Clarkie came upstairs where I was working and asked, 'You wouldn't wanna shoot a few baskets, would you?' He half expected me to say no and was prepared to head back down the stairs without me.

"Instead, I clicked on 'save,' pushed my chair back, and said, 'Sure. Let's go.' He looked wide-eyed and excited, and said, '*Great*. Thanks, Dad!'

"And then he did something wildly impetuous for a nine-year-old boy who is learning to spit and pop wheelies. He hugged me tight and said, 'I love you.'"

Something struck me right about then. It was the look on

my parents' faces. They were both misting up. I don't know what gave me the most joy, what I felt when my son told me "I love you," or my parents' reaction as I told them about their grandson. This closeness, this companionship with my family, was spilling over into a whole platter full of joy.

If you want a definition of the word *joy,* just write out what I felt at the moment in that restaurant, when my mom composed herself enough to say, "You kids have grown up into pretty cool adults."

But I mentioned that this kind of joy has a price tag. What does this joy of parenthood cost? Well, have you ever felt your blood pressure go up because your wife was out and you were at home with the kids?

Let's say she is out for just "a couple of hours" with a friend "to do a *little* shopping," and it turns into five hours of a lot of shopping.

That's a perfect setup for a bad-attitude attack. Rather than stress out, why not veg out? Instead of blowing a gasket, why not shoot a basket? The kids of great dads I know will tell you that they remember with fondness the times their dads got off their high horses and galloped around with them. My parents reminded me of that fact as we continued to swap stories.

Mom got serious and asked, "What things do you remember most about your dad, things that caused you a lot of joy?" She, being a journalist, is always looking for a good story.

I said with a straight face, "Oh, probably the long hours he spent at the office."

Kathey poked me in the ribs and said, "She's *serious.*"

"Mom, Dad," I whined, "she's pickin' on me again."

Then Kathey did her own version of the whine, "Mom, Dad, he's *lookin'* at me again."

Giving up on getting me to "serious up," Kathey took matters into her own hands and turned the dial of the conversation's tone to "Seriously, though." She looked off into the distance and said, "I remember the time Dad took us fishing behind the View Motel in Sedona, and on the way back up to the motel he helped us pick apricots from the tree right behind Grandmother's house."

Her memory jogged one of my own. "I remember the Colorado camping trip when the bear almost ate the birthday cake you guys had for me. Remember that one?"

Did they ever! Dad said, "I had my .22 pistol cocked and under my pillow all night because I thought for sure he was going to come into our tent for that cake." That was news to us. I knew he had brought his gun on that trip but had no idea he was prepared to *use* it. If I had known how scared he was, I probably wouldn't have slept that night, either.

Kathey said, "Remember the November we slogged up the mountain in the mud to cut down that scrawny Christmas tree near Camp Verde? It looked like it should belong to Charlie Brown."

I took a sip of coffee and added, "I recall the week Dad and I spent working on our PHDs together. Remember that, Dad?"

Mom and Kathey exchanged quizzical glances. Dad smiled and added, "Posthole diggers."

"Ah," they both said together.

"Yep. We were putting in fence on Uncle Johnny's ranch, under that blistering New Mexico sun," I said. "And that electric posthole digger thingy…"

"Auger," Dad corrected me.

"Yeah, that electric *auger* posthole digger thingy almost screwed me into the ground."

"And when you wore it out, we had to grab the old-fashioned kind and work that massive upper body of yours."

My sister pinched the muscle on my arm and said, "Oooooh."

The stories went on and on, right through the steak and potato and clear into the apple dumpling with ice cream.

That's the stuff joy is made of. And those stories and that joy cost my dad plenty—plenty of time, plenty of projects that got put on hold for a couple of hours or days, and plenty of grass stains in the knees of his jeans. And yet, as much as it cost him, he'll tell you he wishes he had indulged in frivolity even more often than he did. The cost of joy is high, but the rewards are higher. Almost as high as the loft in our garage.

It came out of the darkness. Something that didn't belong. An odd, squeaky-squally noise that plucked at my subconscious.

I awoke with a start, bumping my head on the rafter just above me.

Rafter? Straining to focus, I realized I was not in my comfortable bed where I usually found myself at odd hours of the morning.

As the squeak grew louder and the adrenaline shot into my brain, I finally remembered where I was, who I was with, and what we were doing. *But what was that noise?* I looked over the edge of the loft in time to see the bottom of the garage door swing out a couple of inches, exposing a thin line of moonlight.

My six-year-old son lay next to me in his sleeping bag, oblivious to the incredible screech of the metal rollers against the track of the heavy wooden garage door that banged shut not once but twice.

I had no flashlight. My son was sleeping with it under his pillow. I had nothing to throw at the intruder expect my pillow. I doubted it would have much impact.

The door swung out again, pulled by something, or was it someone? It was the third time that night I had viewed this strange spectacle. It was as though a spirit were trying to oust us from our perch in the loft "fort" where we slept. Correction: Where my *son* slept soundly and where *I* tossed and turned, staring through the dusky gloom at the garage door below, waiting for this "thing" to come get us.

Finally I caught a glimpse of the little devil. It appeared to be furry and not too big. It was strong enough, however, to pull with its paw at the bottom of the door, which hung above the concrete floor about half an inch.

I spoke to my son to see if he had caught on yet to these strange goings-on. He hadn't. He merely snorted and rolled over, sticking his foot in my face.

The door swung out again, and the beast or animal—whatever it was—almost made it under the eight-inch gap before I used the only weapon I had left—my voice. I yelled, "Get outta here!" (Not very original, but effective.)

It stopped for a moment, stunned that someone would be waiting in its dining room. It never suspected that two brave campers-turned-security-guards would be lying eight feet above its supper.

As it paused in shock, the heavy door swung back, almost

catching its paw in its clutches. It scrambled away as quickly as any animal can.

My heart pounding, I noticed my son's upright silhouette against the pale glow coming from the small window in the side door to the garage.

I said, "I saw it. I think it was a raccoon."

My son's eyes couldn't have been any wider if I'd said, "I think it's a grizzly." This was big-time, high adventure.

Ah, the things we dads do.

No, it wasn't Yosemite. It wasn't the Yukon. But my son and I were braving the elements together—splinters, spiders, gas fumes, hungry animals, head-banging rafters, and all. We did the guy thing. And now we could hold our heads up proudly and tell the women in our family that we had stayed at our posts, never flinching (well, almost never).

It was sort of a rite of passage. Like the survival weekend our Native American friend had told us about. Of course, we hadn't actually lived without food, tools, or clothes for three days in a Colorado wilderness. But we had survived. We were buds. We had become companions in the wilderness. Together. Giving each other courage neither of us had by ourselves.

And as I wrote about this experience in companionship, I remembered the six-year-old pride I had felt after lasting the cold night with my own dad in the northern Arizona woods only thirty-one years earlier. I smiled to myself and looked at my son. He was munching his breakfast toast, watching some silly cartoon on the television in the comfort of our family room.

This was one of those proud moments you never read about in *Reader's Digest's* "Drama in Real Life," but it was dramatic enough for the two of us.

And all because of that silly, macho, male-type demonstration of our affection. We don't mush around with lots of hugs and junk. We just brave the elements together and prove we have what it takes to risk life and limb, if necessary, for our partner.

Ah yes, the things we dads do. For love. Because in our hearts, there is a deep desire to become companions with our kids.

It is the very stuff of joy.

How long has it been since you spent an afternoon with your kids braving the elements of the kitchen or family room? Have you survived a camping experience with one or more of your children? How about a hike in the Grand Canyon or a visit to an air show? Even if your kids are grown, it's not too late to build a few lasting memories.

If it's been a while—especially if it's been a while because you get stressed out by being around your kids—then maybe it's time you learned the art of living large by getting small and "stooping" to their level.

That's exactly what God the Father did for us through Jesus. I love the way Eugene Peterson captures it in his paraphrase of Philippians 2:5–7: "Think of yourselves the way Christ Jesus thought of himself. He had equal status with God but didn't think so much of himself that he had to cling to the advantages of that status no matter what. Not at all. When the time came, he set aside the privileges of deity and took on the status of a slave, became *human!*" (THE MESSAGE).

And that's what we as earthly fathers can do for our kids. We can resist the selfish urges to act like authoritarian kings in our little empires, and we can crawl down off our thrones and act hilariously human with our kids. When I've gotten down to their level, I've seen, from their perspective, how large life can really be.

One afternoon my kids let me look through their eyes at what they valued as *really* important. What brought it into focus was a simple gesture. The gift of a hat.

"Dad, where's your *other* hat?"

My young son's brow was furrowed. "You know, Dad...your FAVORITE one?"

He meant the green-and-white striped one with "#1 DAD" boldly plastered on the front. I hadn't thought it a big deal when I retired that particular hat in favor of my new maize-and-blue hat with the word "Michigan" emblazoned on its front. The Michigan cap with U of M colors was a gift from a good friend who thought I looked "kind of like a train engineer" in the green-and-white one.

"Besides," he said, when he took the other one off my head, "those colors are all wrong." He had this thing for maize and blue. (If you're not a Michigan fan, you might not understand how passionate these people get about green and white vs. maize and blue. They are pretty serious about their colors up here.)

But it *did* matter that I wasn't wearing the green-and-white hat. At least to my kids. It mattered enough to delay our departure for a family outing. Why?

Because the green-and-white one was also a gift, but not from my good friend. It was from my kids. On Father's Day. While other less fortunate fathers were opening ugly ties and stinky colognes, I got a hat.

I proclaimed it my favorite.

And the kids remembered.

They weren't about to let me off the hat hook. While the car idled, they went back into the house...headgear hunting. A sort of small-game chapeau safari. Moments later they emerged with the prized possession. What followed wasn't a formal ceremony. In fact, it only took a few frenetic seconds. But it was as important as the coronation of a king.

My older daughter, Katheryn, yanked off the new hat—the one that fit nicely and almost left me looking like a genuine sports fan—and my son and younger daughter slammed the venerable visor back where it belonged, on dear Dad's cranium. They slammed it on so hard in fact that it made my ears bend down like those of a German shorthaired puppy.

Years ago that hat might have been a crown bestowed on royalty by beloved subjects. This was not just a hat. This was a telling transfer of allegiance.

This "changing of the hats" reminded me of the original significance of the act. It meant that a trio of children had poured pieces of their young souls into an expression, a visible symbol of their extravagant love.

I hadn't really noticed that the only time I wore that hat was on my days off, which meant a bike ride or a walk to the park or a video in the basement, with my kids.

That hat spoke volumes to them. It said, "He's on dad duty. His meter is running. Let's milk some mileage out of him while he's on *our* time." It was an unconscious invitation to stop work, start play, and just be a dad with my kids for a couple of hours.

On my bookcase rests another gift, one with at least equal significance. It's a very unique pen holder with a scale model, cast-metal bulldozer. It used to be parked on a shelf above my father's desk.

Dad was given the pen holder as a reward for doing some engineering work at the Caterpillar proving grounds in Arizona. It was a prized possession of his. He had told me that one day he would pass it along to me.

I grew up, got married, moved away, and forgot all about the bulldozer pen holder.

Until last Christmas.

Now the prize dozer sits on a shelf next to *my* desk. It is, as Stu Weber says, "a sword passed hilt first." It is a crown. It is a visible expression of one heart being united with another heart.

Like in the hat exchange, there wasn't much fanfare in the ceremony, but both symbols carried with them a *huge*-hearted significance.

So despite the fact that I looked "kind of like a train engineer," I left the important green-and-white cap shoved down onto my head, which was now swelling just a little with fatherly pride, and I climbed behind the wheel of the family carriage.

This joy-filled king was taking his loyal subjects on a family outing.

━━═◦๑◦๑◦═━━

I *felt* like a king that day. And I'm sure the reason my kids crowned me wasn't because I had dubbed myself ruler of the family. Quite the opposite. I believe I earned the crown by becoming lowly enough to be like them.

The truth is, my kids are still teaching me what's really noble in this fatherhood job. They continued to recite the formula "joy = companionship" on the day of our nineteenth wedding anniversary.

Toward the middle of the afternoon, Katheryn bounded up the stairs to the office, where I was working (again) at my desk, and announced, "Dad, you can*not* go downstairs for about fifteen minutes, okay?"

"Okay," I said obligingly. She had that twinkle in her eye that told me the kids were up to something. I've learned that mine is not to question why, mine is but to keep my mouth shut and stay glued to the computer while they work their magic.

A few minutes later it was the Calster who bolted up the stairs, and in an excited little whisper she tickled my ear with, "When it's suppertime, you and Mommy have to *not* look in the kitchen after we go get some stuff. But don't tell Clarkie and Katie I told you, okay?"

She almost couldn't stand keeping a secret. The suspense was killing Joy and me, but it was about to cause little Callie to burst wide open and broadcast their plans.

Finally the moment arrived, and at precisely 4:20 P.M. the announcement was made, "We have to go somewhere for a few minutes, and when we get back, we'll tell you when it's safe to come out."

This was getting good.

At the appointed moment, Katie and Callie marched upstairs to escort me down to the kitchen. I discovered that Clarkie was doing the same for Joy, who was downstairs, hiding out in the basement.

We were ushered in from two different doors, with our eyes closed, and then...

"Surprise!" they all three cheered and pointed to the table.

Joy and I looked at the table and at each other and at the kids, and neither of us could believe our eyes.

There, on the table, were two pizzas—not one but two. The first had pepperoni on one side and sausage on the other (they never get sausage, so this was a real sacrifice, for their parents' benefit). On the second we saw ham on one side and bacon on the other. Very versatile pizza. Oh, wow. And bread sticks, too!

They had walked all the way from our neighborhood to Little Caesar's. One quarter of a mile. They had called it in, counted their money, walked up, bought it, and had it waiting for us as our anniversary surprise. We were stunned.

What's more, they had spent their own hard-earned garage-sale money. Lots of it. On *us*.

When we had finished our pizza, they herded us both down into the basement, again to hide while they cooked up Phase Two of their plan. We heard spoons clattering and the freezer opening. Joy whispered, "Dessert." I nodded.

In a few minutes they hauled us up out of the "waiting

room," and there on the table was a beautiful selection of dishes, sundae glasses, "Cloudy, with a Chance of Cookies" ice cream, and spoons. But wait. That's not all. They had also purchased with their own money peanut butter chips, coconut shavings (an odd combination, but not too bad), a small squeeze bottle of Hershey's chocolate, and for the finishing, mouth-watering touch, a little jar of maraschino cherries. Unbelievable!

They giggled and grinned, making Joy and me stay seated while they scooped, poured, plopped, and placed everything just so. And then they served us, reminding us that it was our anniversary and that we were not supposed to do *anything*—with the possible exception of washing the dishes when we were through.

Just when we thought they had pulled every rabbit from their very deep hat, they asked us to adjourn to the living room for the final act of this hilariously moving performance. That's where they presented us with the gifts they had purchased, again with their *own* money, from places all over town.

From The Chocolate Vault (our favorite ice cream hangout after concerts and good report cards) they presented us with two—not one but *two*—varieties of licorice whips, both red and black. In the unmistakable gift bag from Bird & Company Mercantile, we uncovered a sweet little porcelain figurine in the shape of two little Mexican bears, a boy and a girl sitting next to each other with their sombreros pulled down over their eyes. Siesta time, you know. We were told they had names. Joy was the one on the left, and Clark was the one on the right.

Then Callie presented us with her handcrafted masterpiece containing a heart and two people obviously madly in love with each other, as any art critic could tell because of the little hearts drawn all around their eyes.

We figured roughly how much this extravagant display of family affection had cost them. The whole party had to have set them back about ten bucks each. Thirty dollars of pure joy! And they each had made only twenty-five bucks at the garage sale.

When we were all finished with the "official" party, the kids pulled out a wrinkled sheet of notebook paper, which contained their diabolically detailed action plan for "Operation Anniversary."

They had been planning this thing for days, and it read like something from a jewelry-heist movie: 2 P.M., ride bikes to Bird & Co. for gifts. 2:30 P.M., hit The Chocolate Vault. 3:00 P.M., wrap presents. 4 P.M., order pizza. 4:20 P.M., get pizza. 4:30 P.M., eat pizza. They had placed a checkmark next to each item as they had completed the task.

At the very bottom in bold, handwritten print were the words *"Mission Accomplished!"*

Isn't it something, how kids have instinctively known the secret of joy all along? We adults might have grown up and forgotten it, but our kids remind us of what we once knew. Joy— real, lasting, steak-eating, story-swapping joy—is the wonderful lifetime achievement award that results from playful companionship, from investing yourself in someone you love, just for the *joy* of it all!

The steak dinner with my folks and sister and The Secret Anniversary Caper both served as appetizers. They made me hungry for more joy. Chewing on a red licorice whip, breathing in the perfume Callie had sprinkled on her handmade card, I thought, *Life's too short, and kids grow up too fast to miss these moments. I have to tear myself away from the computer more often and not let these magic memories fly by without me. I want to make some more memories while there's still time.*

I'm quite certain that perhaps thirty years from now we'll sit around the table together, maybe even at La Casa Vieja, eating steak and swapping stories. And among the favorite stories told will be the one about the time all three kids spent their garage-sale money to throw a first-class anniversary celebration for two very proud, joy-filled parents.

1. Charles R. Swindoll, *Laugh Again* (Dallas: Word Publishing, 1992), 59.

CHAPTER NINE

At the Heart of Every Great Father
You'll Find Love

—◦◦◦—

Funny, isn't it, how a simple, familiar smell, sound, or sight can flood your brain with detailed memories?

When I was in my midthirties, I remember passing by a young lady in a shopping mall...and catching a whiff of her perfume. Instantly I recalled my first grade teacher, Miss Barr. I could see her! I could remember the layout of the classroom, the freshly painted, Navajo white cinder-block walls, the narrow windows high off the floor, and the slick, painted cement floor. It was so real I could almost smell the crayons and taste the paste.

One little scent and *poof*, there I was at age six, sitting cross-legged on the floor in a circle of children, raising my hand, hoping my beautiful teacher would call on me to pick out a rhythm instrument for music time.

That memory was quickly shut down by another. Miss Barr had to go and marry a dumb old air force captain. Some guys have all the luck. I never even heard what her last name became. Maybe Mrs. Top Gun or something. But that's another story.

A couple of years later, while sitting at my computer in the home office upstairs, I heard a mourning dove cooing its soothing song while perched just outside the window on a telephone wire.

From that simple sound I was transported in my memory to the little church-nursery building off Central Avenue in Phoenix. That's where my parents left me in the nurturing care of Mrs. Palmer, the veteran "baby lady" who wore her hair in a bun and made a mean paper airplane and awesome paper pirate hats.

Those paper creations were supposed to be sailor hats for Noah and the family on the ark, but I thought they looked more like pirate hats. Mrs. Palmer never did go for the patch over one eye. She just couldn't imagine Noah barking out, "Aaargh, me mateys! Swab the deck! Clean up that mess in stall number two!"

I remembered sniffing the freshly mowed grass outside the little building, the pine-scented cleanser used to sanitize the little restroom with the pint-sized potty, and the fresh ink on the mimeographed paper duplicated with enough animal shapes so all us kids could color, cut, and glue a Noah's Ark-sized masterpiece for our parents' refrigerators (which were already listing to starboard from the weight of the previous week's Jonah and the whale projects).

Closing my eyes, I could almost feel the cool linoleum on my skinny little three-year-old legs (I was wearing shorts at the time) as I sat, rolling a little Matchbox car back and forth on the floor's smooth surface.

Amazing, isn't it, how much detail comes into focus, even years after the original experience?

If you'll indulge me for a few minutes, I'd like to lead you on a hike through another highly significant adventure that was brought to mind by a simple gesture. The spark that ignited the memory was the picture I saw when my father took a sip of Chinese tea in a little restaurant in downtown Durango, Colorado.

We were celebrating Dad's seventy-third birthday in the same town where we had vacationed as a family thirty years earlier.

Knowing that my father's muscle movements were being relentlessly bogged down from the insidious effects of Parkinson's, I suggested to Joy and the kids that we take a vacation down memory lane and meet my parents in Colorado. I wanted to retrace the steps of the most incredible vacation I ever took with them when I was about my son's age.

Although it was a real chore for Dad to get up and around, he conquered fatigue and bravely teetered along as we rediscovered many of the same wonder-inspiring things we had enjoyed when I was kid. The best part of the entire trip (for my money!) was the daylong ride on the historic Durango/Silverton narrow gauge train.

The scenery in those magnificent Rocky Mountains defies description, and the old steam locomotive—belching soot and ash—hauls the old-fashioned cars within inches of steep gorges, traveling slowly enough through the passes so camera-toting tourists can lean out windows and snap pictures of the aqua-colored water below. (The two-dimensional photos don't do justice to the real thing.)

It was truly a thrill to vicariously re-experience God's

handiwork by watching my own children's open mouths as they built a lasting memory with their Nana and Dado, just as I had with my parents and grandparents.

A strange and familiar scene took shape in my mind, though, after we had finished the train trip and as we gathered for Chinese food to celebrate Dad's birthday.

Fighting for strength, Dad sat, bent over in his chair at a forty-five degree angle, concentrating on his hand, willing it to pick up the little teacup. He struggled—sweat popping out on his brow—to keep his hand from shaking long enough to catch a quick sip.

That's the instant he triggered the recollection.

That's when the Grand Canyon memory cascaded in like the Colorado River after a heavy, northern Arizona thunderstorm.

In my mind I saw the same hand—shaking with effort—lift a canteen to the same lips. But the reason for the effort was different. It wasn't Parkinson's thirty-two years earlier. It was something I didn't understand until much later, after we were out of the canyon.

In the earlier memory I was only seven years old, the youngest of our little explorers' team made up of my father, then age forty-one, my New Mexico cousins Mickey and Terry, both teenagers, and my sister, age eleven. (She continues to be—and I am quick to remind her of this fact—*four* years older than I am.)

Dad decided we needed to see the Grand Canyon the way *real* explorers had seen it, by foot. We weren't going to take the sissy way out and ride down on donkeys. We would walk, by golly.

And walk we did, all the way down the beautiful and challenging Bright Angel Trail from the South Rim, first through the steep, winding switchbacks, past the Three-Mile Resthouse, on to Indian Garden (the point of no return for us), and through the Devil's Corkscrew until we could see the mighty Colorado below. We crossed the red, rapid river on a footbridge, just like Indiana Jones (though he hadn't been invented yet), and hoofed it across a short stretch to the Bright Angel Campground.

We weren't like "those rich folks" who roughed it in luxurious comfort at the Phantom Ranch. We packed our own, very heavy sleeping bags, which suited us just fine on the canyon floor, dirt and all.

And none of us had to be rocked to sleep that night, since we had successfully navigated 7.7 miles from the top of the trail to the Colorado River and another 1.6 miles to the campground, for a total of 9.3 charley-horsing miles.

At that time in his life Dad had more energy than four guys his age; I felt supremely confident in his ability to guide us through the canyon and out the other side. Now that I'm approaching the age at which he made that trek I wonder what he ate just before he fell asleep and dreamed up such a crazy scheme. Four kids with little hiking experience, the youngest of whom was only seven years old! He must have been watching too many Tarzan movies.

It wasn't his first time in the canyon, though. Because of an earlier successful trip with friends his age, he felt we really needed this life-changing experience while we could still enjoy the untamed wilderness and appreciate God's masterful creation.

My parents had planned well, with plenty of baked beans

and potato salad for the picnic at Grandeur Point on the way to the Trailview starting point. Aunt Jeanie—Mickey and Terry's mom—and my mother would drive the car around to spend the night at some motel. The next day they would do a little sightseeing of their own before greeting us as we triumphantly appeared at the top of the North Rim toward late afternoon on the second day of our journey.

At least...that was the plan.

I remember the pep talks Dad gave us on the drive up. "Drink sparingly. We only have so much water. Don't gulp. Just sip. Take it easy. You may feel strong at first, but you'll need to keep up a steady pace for a long time."

Yada yada yada. I'd heard it all before on our weekend trips around the state. I listened with one ear while picturing myself skinning a bear and decapitating two rattlesnakes with the main blade of my pocketknife.

When we arrived at the trailhead, I kept hopping from rock to rock like a goat. Dad remarked several times that I had more energy than the rest of them, but he hoped I would last until the end. With all those heavy packs, he couldn't carry even the smallest member of his merry band, should any of us need assistance.

The first leg of the journey went by quickly, and the trip to the bottom seemed to fly by. We joked with each other and teased my sister Kathey by saying, "You're doing pretty well...for a *girl.*"

What exhilaration when we finally rounded the corner that gave us our first glimpse of the Colorado River! I wondered what Lewis and Clark felt each time they made a historic discovery. I daydreamed about John Wesley Powell as he rode the frothing Colorado rapids in an old-fashioned wooden boat.

Mr. Powell, the Civil War veteran with a taste for science and geology, was an Arizona hero. We had studied about him in our first grade class, mostly because the school across the street from ours—the one for fourth through sixth graders—was named after him.

I imagined the native Americans, the Hualapai and Havasupai, carving out a living in that awesome canyon carved by the hand of God. And here I was these many years later, an excited seven-year-old explorer with the Grand Canyon to conquer.

Here I am, I thought, *a little kid who has successfully completed the first half of a two-day expedition down the Grand Canyon.* The jubilation throbbing in my imagination far outweighed the throbbing of my calf muscles as I gazed at the stars through the mile-wide slit at the top of this unbelievable chasm.

The next day we awoke just before daylight and feasted on granola. Stretching our legs and tightening our pack belts, we griped about the boring taste of those wretched baked beans, which had long since lost their romance. (To this day, all I have to say to my sister is, "baked beans and potato salad," and she cracks up, remembering the canyon trip.)

Not only did they taste bland, but they were terribly heavy to carry, unlike the ultralight freeze-dried stuff we have available today. We brainstormed a few ways to jazz up the beans: cooked in their can over an open fire, barbecued (although it was hard to keep them from falling through those little cracks), shish-kebabbed (though you could only fit about seven beans on a single toothpick), and our least favorite but most common recipe, cold, straight out of the can.

As we started across the canyon floor, we realized what hadn't really sunk in the day before. We had a much longer journey in store for us the second day.

With each step in that north-by-northeast direction across the relatively flat canyon floor, our feet began to face the fact that our trip out would take almost twice the energy as the walk down.

From the campground to the portion of the Kaibab Trail that climbed steeply to the top was a long, arduous hike across the canyon floor, which was like desert at only 2,480 feet above sea level, almost 5,000 feet below the rim.

The trip out would not be the simple, downhill lope into the canyon. We would have to huff and puff every step of the fourteen miles, with the last five almost straight up.

Dad carefully rationed the water along the way, and when we found some fast-flowing water in Bright Angel Creek, we refilled our canteens. Rangers recommended that hikers carry a gallon of water per person for the trek up the switchbacks, since there were no clean water sources along the final ascent.

As the day grew hotter and our lips grew more parched, it began to dawn on all of us that Dad was right when he said, "Sip, don't guzzle."

All we could think about was getting to the top, drinking as much water as we wanted, and eating a real meal, with no baked beans or potato salad. The older kids talked about how nice a shower would be. That didn't seem all that important to me at the time, but I was definitely interested in a juicy steak for supper.

About halfway up the fourteen-mile trail, one of us remarked, "Hey, we are doing this trip backward. It would have made a *lot* more sense for us to have come *down* the fourteen-mile trail and gone *up* the seven-mile trail." But by then, it was way too late to reconsider.

At the beginning of the day we paused about every hour to take a brief water break and to rest our backs from the heavy packs. Those old-fashioned sleeping bags began to feel like boulders as we hoisted them, all of us leaning forward to balance the weight.

Somewhere along the Bright Angel Canyon, as we crossed a little swaying footbridge suspended over a shallow portion of the creek, my sister let out a screech. We looked back and saw that she had fallen off the bridge into the creek.

"Are you okay, Kath?" my dad yelled.

"I think so," she called back, struggling to right herself.

"Wow, that was pretty good," teased Mickey, "for a *girl.*"

"Did you hit your head?" asked Terry.

"No, I landed on my pack."

Mickey couldn't resist. "Too bad. You would have been saved if you had, since that's the hardest part of your anatomy."

"Ha, ha," replied the now-drenched hiker, who extended her hand and said, "The least you gentlemen could do is give me a hand out of this creek."

I must admit, Kathey handled herself quite well on that challenging hike. As she did in the Grand Canyon, she has faced many ups and downs along the way since then, and with each tumble she's encountered, she has continued to face adversity bravely, tenaciously hanging on to the Lord and pressing on no matter how rough the trail gets. I was then, and am now, secretly quite proud of her. (Don't tell her I said that. It'll ruin my reputation with her.)

Her sleeping bag had become waterlogged, and instead of leaving it behind, my father swapped his sleeping bag with Kathey's so she would have the lighter one.

That was the first time on the entire trip that I realized the hike could actually be dangerous. I had heard reports on the Phoenix news about hikers who had failed to take safety precautions and recklessly barreled into the canyon, thinking they could simply stroll through like a walk in the park. Several had died in accidents and from exposure to the elements.

Plenty of warnings had been given in the brochures we had read, on signs entering the park, and even along the trail. Hats were a must to protect our heads from the rays of the relentless sun. Water was an absolute necessity. And common sense was the order of the day.

As the day progressed, the excitement of the hike gradually degenerated into the drudgery of shuffled feet. Picking points along the trail, we would set little goals for ourselves. "I'm going to walk to that shrub up the trail. Then I'll pick another landmark to shoot for."

On the first day of our hike, on our way down into the canyon, we had passed other weary hikers on their way out. We had remarked to each other about how tired they looked. "Must not have much hiking experience, the wimps," we jested (out of earshot, of course), totally unaware that they would pass their haggard look to our faces the next day.

Stopping for lunch around Ribbon Falls, we dined on another round of those blasted baked beans. We celebrated, however, because we used up the very last can and carried in our packs only the empty (and light) cans, to be thrown away later.

The grandeur of these magnificent falls gave us reason to forget the pain in our backs and legs for a few glorious minutes, and we gawked in a sort of spontaneous reverence at the sight.

I remember thinking, even at age seven, "There *has* to be a God who could make something this incredible. Something this amazing couldn't have just happened."

Then we tore ourselves loose from our resting place and pressed on. Time, we knew, was becoming a critical factor. After another lengthy stretch of trail, all of us caught our second wind as we passed Manzanita Point, where we felt a surge of energy, fueled in part by the last few nibbles of the chocolate candy we had been saving for that rewarding place on the trail.

We set our sights toward Roaring Springs, where we sought a fast-moving place in the stream to fill our canteens one last time before heaving-ho along the trail where we would take a sharp left and start the climb up the most grueling portion of the hike. While filling the canteens, one of our crew (I honestly can't remember which one) dropped a canteen into the creek, and the swift current carried it downstream faster than we could run to catch it.

"That's all right," my dad said with an air of authority. "Just let it go. Don't drown yourselves trying to catch it. Let's just go easy on the water and make it last."

We had made good time across the canyon floor and began to make bets when we would arrive at the top of the trail: "I'll bet you three cans of baked beans we'll get there by 4:30." "Oh yeah? I'll bet you *four* cans we'll get to the top by 4:00!" Mickey would break the silence and lighten the mood every so often. He'd say, loudly, "Hey, Kathey!"

"Hey what?"

"You're still doin' pretty good..." and he'd pause to give us all time to join the refrain, loudly and in unison, "for a *girl*." (Nobody worried about gender harassment in those innocent days—least of all Kathey.)

I began to notice that our breaks were becoming longer and were spaced closer together, some lasting as long as fifteen minutes. I thought, *It's just good old Dad going easy on us little guys,* since he knew we were dog-tired and that the steepest climb lay ahead.

By about the fourth such extended break, though, we all noticed that Dad's color was no longer ruddy. Not only was his face gray, but his breathing had become labored as well. He found a shady shelf upon which to lie down and called us around to give us sobering news. "I want you all to go on ahead and bring your mother and Aunt Jeanie back down with you. I'm not feeling very well, and I really don't think I can go on."

To say we were shocked would be an understatement. My dad *never* complained, and he was *always* the leader, especially on this expedition. Something had to be terribly wrong for him to send us on ahead.

I could tell by the tone in his voice that he wasn't kidding. He was sick. Real sick.

And I was scared.

He gave us that pep talk again about conserving water and pacing ourselves and told us not to worry. *Yeah, right.*

By the mile markers along the trail, I estimated we were about four miles from the rim, and the sun was beginning to sink beyond the canyon wall to our left. I was sure the sun was still shining brightly on the Grand Canyon Lodge at the top, but for us, the energy-draining heat had become a bone-chilling breeze. With each step up the trail as our elevation increased, the temperature decreased. I took a sweatshirt out of my pack and put it on to stave off the shivers.

As the afternoon grew colder and the trail became steeper, I began to pray as fervently as any seven-year-old had ever prayed. *Lord, you have to help us get out of this canyon so we can get help. Don't let my dad die, Lord. Please! Don't let him die.*

Toward the two-mile mark, with only a hint of sunlight left, we heard familiar female voices. "Helloooooooo, down there," they hollered. Fortunately for us they had decided to start down the trail and walk out the last couple of miles with us.

One of my cousins cupped his hands around his mouth and yelled up at my mother and aunt, "Uncle Gaylon is sick. We left him back along the trail."

They laughed.

I couldn't believe it. Here we were, saving my dad from certain death, performing the vital tasks of a rescue party, and the only adults around were laughing!

Then it dawned on me. My father and his brothers and sisters were always pulling pranks and telling jokes, and during the entire car trip to the canyon, Dad had been saying, "I'll probably be the one left lying along the trail somewhere, and these spry young things will bound up to the top of the canyon like antelope."

They thought we had cooked up another great gag. Ha ha ha.

As we hiked up the trail and they down, however, they got close enough to see our faces and hear the tremolo in our voices. It only took a few seconds for them to figure out how serious we were.

We met Dad about a mile back down the trail. He had sucked on a couple of LifeSavers he had found in his pack, and that had boosted his blood sugar level enough for him to make slow, steady, short spurts of progress up the steep, winding trail. He fought with every ounce of energy to cut down the amount of trail left to conquer before getting to the top.

I'll never forget the strange huddle of hikers forming a windbreak in front of my weakened father, who was wearing the Navajo Indian blanket his sister had brought down with her. With my mother at one elbow and Aunt Jeanie at the other, they helped him step after grueling step up the steep switchbacks toward the rim.

Stopping every ten or fifteen minutes, Dad would force his feeble hand to his lips, holding that canteen, trying to sip an ounce or two of that precious, life-giving water.

That was it.

That was the picture that etched itself in my mind, to stay there for years, until Dad drank again in a similar feeble fashion in Durango, Colorado.

One by one, we shed our wide-brimmed hats, since they proved more annoying than helpful now that the sun had completely shrunk away. And one by one, my aunt had placed them on top of each other and on top of her head, until she looked like a character out of a Dr. Seuss book.

Several times, despite the seriousness of Dad's condition, we all burst into nearly hysterical laughter. At least we hadn't lost our sense of humor.

Though we had bet those stupid baked beans we would be out before the sun went down, it was actually well after midnight before we reached the guardrails we had dubbed "the pearly gates" at the North Rim lookout.

When we arrived at the car, Dad was spent. I could tell by the look on my mother's face that she feared he had succumbed to what he had repeatedly warned us about—heatstroke. It could be deadly.

And besides the dehydration, which was bad enough, he had endured strong winds and cold temperatures at the higher elevations, which added to his physical exhaustion. He was almost in a state of hypothermia.

We had eaten virtually everything in our packs, and my mom and aunt had not stocked up on food since they thought we would have plenty of time to drive to a nearby store and buy sandwich material.

The only thing worth eating in the car was a small bag of red delicious apples, which my aunt sliced and rationed out. Dad tried to eat a slice but was so tired he could barely chew.

I gulped down my five slices and fought off hunger pangs. I tried not to beg, though, since I knew Dad was in serious shape and there was nothing to be done about it until we found a place that sold food and water.

We drove several miles toward the Utah border, stopping at a tiny, cabinlike grocery store, where it was obvious the owner lived in a room next to the store. My normally reserved aunt banged on the door of his tiny house until the extremely sleepy and not-too-friendly-looking, weather-wrinkled, skinny little fellow opened the door.

Desperate times call for desperate measures, and my aunt paid a whopping five bucks for a loaf of bread, a jar of peanut butter, and some drinking water—outrageous prices for 1964. I was so hungry even a peanut butter sandwich tasted good.

I drifted off to sleep in the backseat of the faded blue Chevy station wagon, praying silently, *God, please, please let my dad be okay.*

Hours later—though it felt like seconds—I awoke to the smell of bacon frying. Birds chirped outside a strange window through which a shaft of sunshine penetrated. I took a sniff and caught the familiar smell of pine after a gentle morning rain. I opened an eye in an effort to determine where I was.

It turned out to be a cabin near Kanab, a little town just north of the Kaibab National Forest, barely across the Arizona border in Utah, where my uncle had met us. I stumbled sleepily out of bed, rubbed my aching legs, and shuffled into what I thought must be the kitchen, following the directions my nose provided.

There, much to my amazement and relief, was my dad, sitting at the kitchen table, breathing in the deep aroma of his coffee. His face had that characteristic reddish brown coloring, and although he looked as weary as a mule after plowing, he was very much alive.

A simple gesture, like the sipping of a little liquid, brought back all those memories and in such detail. Yet I hadn't thought about them for years.

It was a similar, simple gesture that brought back a flood of memories on another dusty trail. This one was not located in the Grand Canyon. It was, however, on a road about the same length as the Bright Angel trail was from the South Rim to river, seven and a half miles. This trail carried travelers from Jerusalem to a little waterhole called Emmaus.

Another hike revealed two travelers who shuffled as they walked, shoulders bent, faces dejected. They talked of sadness, worry, doubt, fear, and confusion as they prayed fervently and pressed on.

These two heavyhearted hikers had traveled the emotional switchbacks starting with the initial excitement as they followed their leader into grandeur. They had been filled with excitement and wonder and had stood silently in reverence at the awesome acts of God. But then they saw their hopes dashed as their leader, Jesus Christ, had fallen.

They had heard the reports from the women who had run to the tomb early on the first day of the week, only to find it empty.

They might have speculated about the women's report: "They must be dreaming. Wishful thinking maybe? How could it be? Was the body stolen? Did the soldiers do this to mock us? What has happened to Him? What will happen to us?"

They might have even talked about the last words Christ spoke on the cross and about how much He must have suffered in His final hours. What had He said in those final moments? "I thirst"?

Being thirsty themselves, they must have thought, *How awful for Him to be so parched and with nothing to quench it.*

We thought He was the King, and yet...maybe He was just

a man. A human being who gets thirsty like the rest of us.
They had seen the glory of the kingdom but failed to see the
purpose in the suffering. God hadn't done for them what they
wanted Him to.

Knowing the Old Testament as they did, they no doubt
quoted prophecies and wondered aloud how they could not be
true, given the unusual ending to this story, which was supposed
to have ended in a new King leading God's people to freedom.

Then, somewhere along the trail, the travelers looked
behind them to see who was causing the *slap, slap, slap* of a
third set of sandals. A third traveler appeared along the road
and began walking at their pace.

"What are you guys talking about?"

"Don't you know what's been happening? It's front page
news! You must be the only one around here who doesn't
know what's been goin' on in Jerusalem."

"Tell me about it."

"Well, this man had become very well known, a great
leader. His name was Jesus. Some called Him the Nazarene.
Everyone was so sure that this guy was the one they had been
waiting for, the one who would become King. He was a
prophet, a man of God, and a highly inspirational speaker. So
dynamic. He did great things for people, not for money, but
just because He wanted to help them."

"Yes, and…?"

"And He was *killed*. Right when we thought He was
about to make His move. Dead," and the man drew his thumb
across his throat to make his point, "just like that. Our high
priests and leaders betrayed Him, trumped up some charges,
and sentenced Him to death. And," they shook their heads as

they paused to collect their thoughts, "they...well, they crucified Him.

"We were positive this was the One told about in the prophecies. We'd studied those passages since we were kids. They all seemed to add up, you know? We had our hopes up that this was the guy who was going to deliver Israel. But it's been three days since all these terrible things happened and there's still not a sign of Him anywhere, except for these crazy reports from those emotional women."

The traveler continued to walk with them, probing with a simple question: "What do *you* think happened?"

"We don't know what to think anymore."

The stranger looked into the eyes of the two grief-stricken travelers. "Why can't you believe what you have just been quoting, all those things spoken by the prophets?"

No answer. Just the sound of sandals slapping the sun-baked trail.

"Don't you think it's possible that these things had to happen, that they were all part of the plan you've just discussed? Don't you think there might be some purpose in all of this? That all the suffering had to take place for the pieces to fit together? That the Messiah had to suffer and die in order to enter into His glory? That God was trying to show the world something about Himself?"

The two original travelers exchanged quizzical glances but still made no reply.

Answering their silence, the third man began rehearsing the prophecies, starting way back at the beginning, with the Books of Moses, and continuing with all the familiar passages of the Prophets, pointing out all the landmarks of Scripture that referred to Jesus as the Messiah.

Just as he was finishing this discourse they came to the edge of the village, where he said, "Well, this is the fork in the trail, gentlemen. It's been a pleasure." And the stranger started off toward the next town.

One of the two travelers spoke up. "Wait. It's getting late—and you've walked a long way. You really ought to come over to our place and rest a bit. Have a bite to eat."

The other hiker chimed in, "Yeah, please stay just a little longer, and at least put up your feet for a while. Our house is just around the corner."

With a grateful nod, the third walker changed directions and motioned for his new friends to lead the way. Once inside the house, when they sat down to eat, the third fellow smiled at His hosts, picked up a piece of flat, round bread, and tore off a couple of pieces, handing them to the men seated across the table from Him.

Again, the two men exchanged glances as their eyebrows rose simultaneously.

Then the fellow picked up a clay cup that had been filled with wine and slowly, purposefully, lifted it to His lips.

A simple gesture let loose a river of dammed-up memories and revealed something so profound they nearly dropped their food.

The two men started talking at once, almost falling over their guest. "Master, it *is* You! I can't believe it. Why? How? When? And all this time we were walking with... How can this *be*?"

Then He disappeared. Just like that. Gone.

"Whoa," they both said. They sat staring at the place where He had just been. "Whoa." And they both just breathed a few times, shaking their heads.

Then, again, they both began falling all over themselves, making plans to return to Jerusalem, grabbing a few items to take with them on their hurried trip back the seven and a half miles to tell the others.

"Can you believe it?"

"He was right there."

"And all those things He was saying. We *knew* those passages."

"Didn't you feel something different—something strange—when He was quoting those scriptures? I mean, it was like being right *with* Him. Well, shoot, it *was* being with Him. I mean He was THERE!"

"C'mon, let's go. I can't wait to see the looks on their faces when we tell them..."[1]

Isn't it just like Jesus to reveal Himself in a simple gesture rather than a huge explosion? The two travelers learned a valuable lesson about the purpose of His suffering. He had to become thirsty in order for them to have Living Water.

Jesus said, "He who drinks of this water will never be thirsty again."

He loved them enough to give Himself up on their behalf. He was their living water.

Oh yes, there is one other thing I should mention about the Grand Canyon trip. I discovered this fact on the third day after our adventure had begun. As we rehashed the events of the trek, my father made a startling admission.

"After the canteen got lost down the creek, I got a little

worried about you kids having enough water. I decided to help us conserve a little more than before, so I stopped drinking."

Terry spoke up, "But, Uncle Gaylon, we saw you drinking from the other canteen."

"Well, I wasn't really drinking. I was only pretending to drink. I didn't want you guys to worry."

Whoa. I had seen the glory of the canyon but had failed to see the purpose behind the suffering.

Three days after our journey had begun the purpose became clear. He had become thirsty so we could have life-giving water. And that's why such a simple gesture revealed something so profound. A sip of tea in a Chinese restaurant in Durango, Colorado, brought back a flood of memories about a father who taught us a grand lesson about the Son.

At the heart of every great father is the willingness to sacrifice for the sake of his kids. That's what the Father did through His Son, Jesus. He gave the ultimate sacrifice so we could live. He gave Himself. He became thirsty so we would never have to thirst again. He took the journey into death so that we could take the journey into life.

At the heart of every great father is *that* kind of love. A grand, awe-inspiring love profoundly motivated by the Holy Spirit, making it possible for a dad to pour himself out for his kids.

1. Luke 13–34. I have loosely paraphrased this passage for dramatic purposes. The actual passage doesn't include some of the details I've speculated about. For example, Jesus simply broke the bread, and in that act the two men recognized Him. It was not in the act of drinking, as I suggested in this dramatized version. I just couldn't resist bringing in the simple act of drinking as the identifying gesture, since it fit so well with the Grand Canyon story. Please forgive me for my storytelling license, and please take time to read the real story for yourself. There's no replacement for the actual passage of Scripture!

CHAPTER TEN

At the Heart of Every Great Father
You'll Find Jesus Christ

—=*ひ/ひ/ひ*=—

The engine slowed, sputtered, and backfired as the air-speed indicator needle wavered between sixty and sixty-four miles an hour. The wind whistling through the guy wires between the upper and lower wings suddenly went silent, just as the left wing dipped toward terra firma and the nose dropped like a granite boulder.

My eyes darted from the altimeter—which hung for an agonizing split second at twenty-nine hundred feet—to the horizon, which suddenly shot upward as the nose plummeted downward. My next view was of the farmer who had heard the backfiring engine and was now standing next to the tractor that had been pulling his hay wagon.

I imagined him with his mouth wide open, considering which way he should run.

With the 1941 Stearman biplane's left rudder pedal pushed all the way to the front, the "Black Baron" dropped into a steep counterclockwise spin, with the farmer in the exact center of the circle, no doubt thinking he'd be picking up more than bales of hay in a matter of seconds.

Seminary had never prepared me for *this*.

Because I was strapped into the open cockpit with an over-the-shoulder nylon harness and a more traditional seat belt cinched tight, I thought, *There's no way I can unhook all this stuff and use the parachute strapped to my body before we hit the ground.*

Since from my perspective the plane was the only stationary thing, it looked as though someone had grabbed the edge of the farm below and spun it clockwise. My stomach levitated somewhere between my liver and lungs.

The little plane plunged like a diving hawk. I counted one full revolution and then peeked at the altimeter. Twenty-one hundred feet and falling.

After another half spiral the engine growled back up to speed, and seconds after the plane stopped flying and started falling, gravity mysteriously and wonderfully reasserted itself inside the cockpit as my leg muscles tensed to support my body's weight on the wooden foot runners in the fuselage.

As quickly as he had appeared, the farmer disappeared from my view. The world tilted downward out of sight, and the horizon magically took shape before me—the glorious Michigan clouds creating a dark-gray canopy above. I can't remember when I was that happy to see those ugly clouds. A quick glance below the left wing revealed that, yes, we were indeed flying parallel to the ground and not perpendicular to it.

The altimeter now showed a steady seventeen hundred feet. *We had dropped twelve hundred feet in less than five seconds.* The plane climbed steadily to two thousand feet and leveled off. The great relief expressed as I shouted "Eeee-HAW!"

was swallowed up in the engine noise and wind in that grand, cloud-filled expanse of sky.

I glanced to my left, at the little circular mirror mounted on the main wing strut, and saw the edges of the thick mustache turn upward toward the old-fashioned goggles held tight against the face of Bob Barden, master pilot and stunt-flyer. He pulled the machine-gun trigger on his stick, causing the earphone over my left ear to snap, crackle, and pop to life.

His voice, mixed with static and pride, asked, "How was *that?*"

Deeply inhaling the moist September air—in love with a life that had just flashed before my eyes—I grinned broadly and thrust my left hand above the cockpit in front of the little mirror. My thumb pointed triumphantly into the air.

Just then the tiny windshield began streaking with droplets of water, and Bob's voice crackled again into my earphone. "We're getting a little sprinkle. Better head back to the tower."

I nodded, relaxed my leg muscles for the first time in twenty minutes, and watched the miniature farms pass below as we banked steeply to the left and then followed Highway 12 northeast, past Saline, and on toward the Ann Arbor airport.

So..., I said to myself, *that's what a recovery maneuver feels like!*

"What about pilots?" asked Ed Gore.

I had just told him my idea for the last chapter of the book. This book. I said, "Ed, I'm looking for an analogy, some experience that would illustrate how a dad can turn around his life and head back in the right direction."

I admitted I was afraid readers would think I had it made, growing up in a *Leave It to Beaver* household with no major problems. I wanted them to know that my dad broke away from his past when he left home for college. I wanted them to understand that my father struck out into the frightening, unknown wild blue yonder when he chose to believe that Christ really was the Son of God, courageously setting his compass to a different heading than the one his father had used.

"Some of the guys reading this book will come from homes where the examples of fatherhood aren't real great," I explained. "But I want to demonstrate to them through an exciting story that a man—*any* man—can turn things around and head in the right direction. I want them to know they can start a new branch on their family tree—like my dad did for me and my sister."

That's when Ed suggested the flight analogy. "Do you know any fighter pilots, Clark? I've heard they learn certain maneuvers that enable them to scream their jets around quickly, especially when they're dogfighting with an enemy."

That was the bright idea that eventually led me to Mike Mullikin, the friend of a friend, and a former marine fighter pilot.

Joy and I met Mike the first time at a table in the back room of the Country House Restaurant where the owner had set us up, away from the incoming lunch crowd. Across from us a youthful, polite, and quietly animated gentleman with red hair and a ruddy, Irish complexion spoke with precision and clarity as he described several maneuvers from a jet pilot's perspective.

"When you learn the basic maneuvers, you do everything by the numbers," he said, pointing to the three-inch-thick F-4 Flight Manual he had brought along to loan me so I could read about the fighter.

Mike's expertise and knowledge awed me. It stunned me to realize this guy had flown "The Double Ugly" F-4, a fleet defender used to protect aircraft carriers against attack and to protect the guys on the ground.

I could hardly believe that this youthful fellow—not that much older than I, I estimated—had flown this multimillion-dollar weapons platform at almost astronautical altitudes and at more than two times the speed of sound, landing on a postage-stamp-sized carrier in the middle of an ocean and dropping his catch hook to be snagged by a cable quicker than I can park my Toyota wagon in the garage.

Mike painted such vivid word pictures about his flight experiences that I must have leaned in my chair, adjusting the aileron to roll into level flight. I saw a glint in his eyes as he talked with passion about something he did extremely well. After his stint in the service, he began flying commercially and now flies 757s for Northwest Airlines.

"Doing these maneuvers by yourself and by the book is one thing," he said, "but it gets a little more tricky when there's an enemy—or two or three—in the three-dimensional air around you."

He demonstrated with a little bronze airplane paper-weight. "When you dogfight, the main thing is to keep your turns tight and your energy up. If you get too aggressive and go into a turn with too much energy, it takes longer for the plane to come around, and the enemy can turn tighter than you, come in on your inside, and shoot you down." He flew a salt shaker in a tighter turn than the paperweight and killed the bronze airplane before our eyes.

"Sounds like fatherhood," I said. "Power with restraint."

He laughed. "Exactly."

I couldn't help but add, "When I've gone into a discipline maneuver with one of my kids with too much energy—when I've gotten too aggressive—I've flown out of bounds, and the old enemy flies in and kills my example of patience and self-control."

"Yeah," Mike winced a little, "I can relate to that, too. I find it easier to act with great patience around other people's kids, but when I get home with the ones I love the most, it's easy to let my guard down and treat them worse than I treat total strangers."

We were connecting on this fatherhood-analogy stuff. My new friend took our conversation to an even higher altitude.

"When we were taught what to do if we got disoriented, we were given three rules of thumb based on simple, common sense. When you lose your sense of direction…

1) *keep flying the plane,*
2) *find a landmark or the horizon,*
3) *and talk to someone.*

"When guys lose their cool," he explained, "they forget the basics. They forget they have to have enough altitude, air speed, and energy to keep the plane flying! If they start trying to wrestle the thing around where they think they ought to go, or if they start flapping their jaw when they should be thinking, they throw themselves into a spin or fly into a mountain or into the ground."

I thought, *Yeah, and when we dads lose our cool, we need to remember the basics. We need to keep flying by the numbers instead of flying off the handle. If we could only remember to keep enough energy in our fathering to act patient, with self-control, with gentleness, when we feel like panic or fear or anger is taking control, then maybe we could keep from driving a good lesson into the ground, exploding the chance for a good instructional moment.*

Mike continued, "The next thing we were taught to do is to look for a landmark. Once you've found something to keep your eye on, it's easier to get your sense of direction, and you can figure out where you are in relation to the ground."

I thought, *Like when we forget to keep our eyes on Christ, the One who is immovable. By focusing on Him, we can maintain our sense of direction.*

"And after you've made sure you're still flying and after you find your landmark, *then* you talk to somebody. You get on that radio and ask for assistance."

By now my brain was popping with analogies. I thought, *We guys have a tendency to be lone rangers. Wouldn't it be great for us to simply talk to somebody when we've lost our sense of direction?*

Great advice on flying in battle.

Great advice on fatherhood.

I scribbled notes furiously as Mike talked. Then, just as I was about to look up from my notepad for another great analogy, he dropped his bombshell.

"I could talk all day about this stuff—pilots love to talk about flying—but in order for you to write about these maneuvers with feeling, I think you need to *experience* some of 'em."

Uh-oh. I had a strange premonition he was thinking of something more than a commercial flight to Des Moines.

"I'd like to give you a gift," Mike told me. "I'll pay for a flight with Bob Barden, a friend of mine who flies a stunt plane at air shows."

Stunt plane? Air show? My eyes got wide, and I exhaled very slowly.

"Wow," I said, blinking. At that instant I didn't know what else to say.

"Yeah. He does all these maneuvers I've told you about, but at slower speeds than in a jet."

Right. Like about five times slower. And a *lot* lower to the ground.

"That's incredible," I said.

"So what do you think?" he asked.

"Wow," I said.

And all this because I wanted a simple analogy for dads who can turn their lives around and head back in the other direction, flying straight and level. Well, ask, the Man said, and you shall receive.

"That looks like your plane," Mike exclaimed as we turned left at the first hangar inside the gate of the Ann Arbor airport. My heart started beating a little faster.

I looked at this vintage aircraft and saw "The Black Baron" painted on the fuselage. There she was, sitting on the apron just outside a paint-peeled hangar.

She was a barnstorming beauty, just like the ones I'd seen in the books I'd checked out from the public library. Looking at this open-cockpit, two-seater biplane took you back to the days when Charles Lindbergh had delivered mail all over the Midwest. This was quite possibly the same type of airplane in which my father had flown when he was a kid—after he traded a live chicken for a ride.

I wondered if I could trade a chicken *not* to ride. Noticing the clouds rolling in from the west, I also remembered reading that Lindbergh had bailed out a couple of times when the fog got so thick he couldn't see to land. I tried to put that thought out of my mind as my stomach muscles shivered a bit.

The plane was obviously not your stock Stearman, flown right off the showroom floor. It had a spectacular black-and-white sunburst design painted on the wings and a racy cowling for increased aerodynamics. The rudder was an eye-catching black-and-white checkerboard, with a single white cloverleaf growing out of a black field just above the tail fins.

She also sported a couple of small ailerons added to the upper wings so Bob could snap around quickly with quarter rolls and barrel rolls, and so the plane would respond with split-second accuracy.

Two weeks earlier I'd had no idea who Bob Barden was or that such a plane even existed in Ann Arbor. I was about to get to know him quite well, however.

I was about to trust this man with my life.

Inside the hangar a couple of old chairs sat near a weather-beaten Steelcase desk. Behind that desk sat a trim, silver-haired man looking at some paperwork. He spun around with the enthusiasm of a man twenty years his junior, and almost before we could say, "You must be Bob," he called out, "Hello, fellas! You must be Mike and Clark."

This guy exuded as much energy as his plane produced noise. From the moment I greeted him, I liked him. His personality was young, charming, humorous, joyful. And he was a perfect gentleman. He reminded me a little of B-movie heart-throb Don Ameche, with his silver mustache and a ready smile.

Bob had been flying stunt shows for more than twenty years and was in competitions before that. He handed me a promotional flier, which noted that he usually opened his act with an inverted flat spin, descending vertically straight down over a mile and turning as many as twenty times. I suppressed another shiver.

He told us that the Boeing Stearman had been beefed up from a standard 220-horsepower engine to a powerful 450-horse. "You need the extra oomph," he explained, "to get up and over in these tricks." In order to do stunts for an audience on the ground, Bob had a special clearance from the FAA that allowed him to fly these maneuvers below fifteen hundred feet. "Nobody would think they were very spectacular if you were only a dot in the sky," he said matter-of-factly.

I asked Bob to explain some of his maneuvers. He told me about the flat spin, referred to as a "recovery maneuver," the crop-duster turn, and the hammerhead. I asked about the "Immelman," since Mike had explained that one before.

"Oh yeah," he said, "we do that, too. We'll get our speed up to about 140 miles an hour, yank back on the stick, and fly up and over until we're upside down. Don't worry though; you'll be strapped in, so you shouldn't fall out."

"Oh good," I said.

"Then we'll just roll right over onto our belly and away we'll go, in the opposite direction."

That was the maneuver—the Immelman—that really piqued my attention. Imagine flying 140 miles an hour in one direction, then—in a matter of scant seconds—you've flipped around so that you're flying on the opposite heading. What if life could be like that?

After I had sufficiently pestered him with questions for a half-hour, Bob asked *the* question. "Well," he smiled, "are you ready to fly?"

Mustering as much enthusiasm as I could, I answered, "You betcha! But...umm, you wouldn't happen to have a restroom around here, would you?"

"Good idea," he laughed.

Returning to the hangar, I took out my wallet and keys, saying, "My insurance card is in here, Mike. And my blood type is B-negative."

Bob grabbed a parachute and said, "Here, let me help you on with this rig."

My legs were beginning to shiver, and not from the cold. I kept taking deep breaths through my nose and tried to look completely relaxed. Bob said, "Now, if I tell you to jump, you really need to do that. Otherwise, you'll be the lone pilot in that thing," and he glanced over toward the plane.

I looked up from the straps to see if he was laughing. He wasn't.

We walked to the plane, and Bob said, "Now, just step up onto that black area on the lower wing and climb over into the front cockpit. Step only on that solid area, though, because the wing is made of paper."

Oh great. Paper wings.

Bob snapped his fingers and said, "Oh yeah, I'll go get you

a helmet." He walked back into the hangar. I guess I'd watched too many *Top Gun*–type movies, because I expected some high-tech helmet with built-in microphone and a visor. What Bob brought out, however, was a canvas and Velcro affair that made me look like Snoopy playing the part of the Red Baron.

Bob asked once more if I was all set and then said, "When we get airborne, you can talk to me by pulling the machine-gun trigger on your stick. Pull it and hold it while you talk, then release to listen. But don't talk to me through the intercom until we're clear of the tower, otherwise they'll hear what we're saying to each other." I nodded. He practically shouted, since my earphones muffled much of the sound. I was glad for that, because when he started the 450-horsepower Prat and Whitney, the noise was incredible, even with the earphones on. A huge cloud of smoke blew out the exhaust when the engine cranked the propeller into motion.

Mike gave me a thumbs-up with a questioning look on his face that beckoned, "Are you up for this?" I grinned and gave him the "okay" sign with my right hand. Bob sat behind me for several minutes, going through his checklist. He moved his stick in all directions, making sure all the interconnected mechanical parts were responding as they should.

Then, after exchanging several bits of gibberish with the tower, he gunned the throttle, and we began to taxi toward the runway. With Mike quickly fading from sight, he gave me an official, fighter pilot marine salute.

I saluted back. *Here we go,* I thought.

—⟨o/o/o⟩—

The Black Baron roared down the runway, picking up speed as Bob "drove" forward for what felt like two hundred yards. He handled the plane so smoothly I could hardly tell when we actually lifted off the ground. Once we were completely clear of the runway, he gently pulled back on the stick, and we edged easily up and over the trees past the airport.

Bob banked us toward the southwest, and we headed straight down Highway 12, a familiar route for me since I had driven it from Ann Arbor to Tecumseh at least a hundred times. We headed for the open fields north of Tecumseh where aerobatics are legal—presumably since there are fewer houses to crash into.

"Why don't we start with a loop—just so you can get the feel of being upside down?" he said. Even through the headset I could barely understand him because of the wind, noise, and static. I nodded up and down, forgetting I could now talk to him through the intercom.

"I'm gonna pick up some speed, then I'll pull straight up. Don't forget to grunt as we pull up because you'll be pulling about four Gs. Okay?"

I nodded again and pulled one more time on the straps holding me into the seat. "Oh boy," I said aloud to the control panel.

The engine began to rev even higher, and the speed indicator showed we were racing toward 120 miles an hour. I could tell we were in a shallow dive, no doubt to pick up the speed he needed to get up and over.

"Let's show these folks on the highway what a loop looks like," Bob said. "If we do this right..." and he paused for effect, flashing that patented grin in the mirror, "then we should come out facing exactly the same direction, at precisely the same point we started. Here we go!"

I watched the speed increase to 130, then 135. Then exactly as the needle reached 140, the "phantom stick" in front of me shot back toward my seat, and I began to feel my weight increase dramatically. The horizon tilted, and I grunted and strained to keep the blood at the top of my body.

Remembering what Mike had said about a landmark, I looked over my left wing and could still catch a little of the horizon below me as it faded from sight, since we were now pointed straight up. I had to strain my neck muscles in order to look to my left. My body felt like it weighed 560 pounds, but only for a couple of seconds. The pressure from centrifugal force eased up after we began to arch back and over. I threw my head back and immediately saw the opposite horizon far below me. I chose a farmhouse below as my landmark, and just as Mike had said, looking at that steady object kept me from feeling completely disoriented. I knew where we were by being in relationship with the landmark.

As we reached the top of the loop, I felt almost weightless for a split second, and the straps over my shoulders tightened just a bit. Then the seat below me pushed up against my tightened hams as we zoomed down and headed straight toward the ground. Directly below us (which meant directly in front of us, since we were pointed straight down) there was Highway 12, exactly where we had left it a few moments earlier!

I felt more pressure against the seat as the Gs from the circle increased on the bottom quarter of the loop, and soon we were flying straight down the highway, just as when we began.

Bob asked through the intercom, "How are you feeling?"

I grinned gamely at the mirror and gave him a thumbs-up.

"If you feel the slightest discomfort, don't hesitate to let me know," he said. Ever the gentleman.

"Shall we try a barrel roll, so you can experience a couple of negative Gs?" he asked.

Remembering I could talk through the tiny microphone stuck at the end of a curved wire jutting out of my left earphone, I reached forward, found the switch at the top of the stick, pulled it, and said, "Sounds great. This is terrific!"

Bob smiled. "We'll roll left so you'll know which direction to look. Hang on." He put on his serious stunt-pilot face, checked all his dials, and then executed a perfect roll, all the way around, in one fluid motion—something that takes real skill, considering that you have to fly the plane sideways, then upside down, then sideways again, then around to normal while constantly adjusting the ailerons and keeping the plane angled when it's upside down so it doesn't flip over and head straight toward the ground. It was obvious he had done this a few times. For that, I was grateful.

I kept my eyes on a barn through most of the maneuver and felt only a slight discomfort as we hung upside down in our harnesses. Bob could tell by my face that I was really having a great time, so he was eager to show me more tricks.

He performed a cloverleaf, which consists of four consecutive loops, with a quarter twist on the way down out of each one. He followed this up with a crop-duster turn and a "hammerhead."

I was beginning to get into this. "That was great!" I shouted into the microphone.

"How about that flat spin?" Bob asked. "Ready for that one?"

"Go for it!" I yelled.

"We'll need some altitude, so it'll take a minute to climb."

The plane responded to his touch like a fiddle becoming a violin. We climbed for a little over a minute, reaching a height of twenty-nine hundred feet. That's when I experienced the flat spin—the *recovery maneuver* described at the beginning of this chapter—followed by the "Immelman," which set us on a straight and level course.

Man, what a thrill! There is nothing quite like being in a plane when it just quits flying. I'm sure Bob would have gladly pulled a few more maneuvers out of his bag of tricks, but the rain that began to streak the windshield drove us back to the runway in Ann Arbor.

And all that because I wanted an exciting analogy to help dads!

You'd better be careful what you pray for.

"Did you get what you needed to write the chapter?" asked Mike on the way to Chi Chi's for lunch and a debriefing session. Did I ever.

As we munched on chips and salsa I told him, "I had no idea how much work goes into flying."

"Almost as much as goes into being a dad," he replied. "Just don't tell anyone how much fun it is. We commercial pilots like the folks in the plane to think we're working real hard up in the cockpit."

We talked about our families, laughed about some of the funny things our kids had done, and then I told him a little about my dad. "You know, I think I could call my dad an 'Immelman Dad.' When you think about it, he pulled quite a 'recovery maneuver' when he struck out in a new direction after leaving home for college. His dad—my other grandfather—didn't have the fatherhood thing down pat. He was a pretty rough character...a Wild West cowboy with all the habits to boot.

"I really enjoyed visiting that side of the family, but as I grew up, I recognized how different my dad was from the rest of the family. My dad could have flown in a very different direction—and grown up doing a lot of the things my grand-dad did. And if he had, *my* life would have been very different. All of those Spirit-filled character qualities I'm trying to get across in my book might have been out of my reach."

For a moment, I felt the excitement surge up within me. "But Dad did an Immelman! When he trusted Christ, he pulled back from his past, rising above his circumstances. God gave him the strength to turn things completely around. He started flying straight and level and *kept* it straight and level."

Mike was intent. He nodded thoughtfully. "It took a lot of courage for your dad to do that. He really took a risk, didn't he?"

"Yes he did. In fact, for several years he was about the only believer in his immediate family, except his mother, who had been praying that her kids would come to know Christ."

Mike added more spice to the conversation as we added more salsa to the dip bowl. "I've made some mistakes in my past, Clark...and I've been reading a book that is helping me learn not to listen to the negative talk inside my head. I'm learning it's okay for me to let go of my past and to head boldly into the future. Sounds like that's what your dad did."

"Yep. He started that branch of the family tree growing in a new direction. And over the years, many of his brothers and sisters have come to know Christ, too."

Mike nodded. "That's great."

The waitress brought us our lunch, I prayed for the Lord to help keep it in my stomach, thanked Him for a great experience and a new friendship, and we dug in. Mike laughed, "If you can hold two enchiladas down after all those maneuvers, you're doing all right!

"By the way," he asked, "which maneuver was the most dramatic to you?"

"It's a tossup," and I paused to act nauseous for a moment, playing on the words, and he laughed again. Then I continued, "...between the hammerhead and the flat spin."

"Oh yeah. That spin is really uncomfortable the first time you experience it."

"You know it," I said. "When the bottom drops out, it feels like it's all over but the benediction. It looked like we were going to drill a well on Old McDonald's farm with the propeller."

Because Mike had warned me about that maneuver before I had gone up with Bob, I had braced myself. What I discovered from Bob after the flight, however, really lit my afterburners.

When I got my legs to work again after we landed, I asked him, "How would you get out of the spin if you stalled unintentionally?"

"The best thing to do is to let go of the stick," he said, motioning a complete release with his hands.

I was shocked. "You're kidding!"

"Nope. When you let go, the ailerons line themselves up with the wings, and you can then pull back on the stick and fly out of the spin. Some guys try to *wrestle* it back into flight— and they only wind up flying into the ground. That's why the maneuver is nicknamed 'the pilot killer.'"

Here was another of those amazing analogies I was hoping for. I thought, *Just like in fatherhood. You lose momentum— maybe even stall out in your marriage or with your kids—and it feels like the bottom drops completely out. But the more you try to muscle it back into smooth air on your own strength, the worse it gets, until you fly it right into the ground.*

I told Mike about this idea at the restaurant. "Isn't that just like the paradoxical truth about Spirit-filled fatherhood? The best way to get back on the right track is to simply let go of the stick..."

Mike finished the sentence for me, "...and let the Holy Spirit do the work for you! I'm still working on that one, Clark. Seems like you just get a grip on some parts of the job only to have 'em slip away from you. I'm glad God keeps flying me out of the spins I put myself into."

"Me too, Mike. Me too."

For me to try to get better as a dad without submitting my life to the control of the Master Mechanic, the Holy Spirit, would be just as silly as Bob trying to get better performance from his

Stearman by putting an extra coat of wax on the fuselage. You have to get under the cowling before the plane is changed where it needs to be changed.

Until I let God get into the inner workings of my life—deep down where my motives fire up my actions—I'm just trying to fly out of a flat spin by wrestling with the stick. It's not only frustrating. It's deadly.

It's impossible for me to exercise self-control until I have Jesus becoming Lord over that area of my life. There's no way I can be gentle with my kids when they're driving me crazy if I haven't surrendered my boisterous behavior to Christ.

All the other fruits of the Spirit described in this book become an exercise in fatherhood failure when I try to accomplish them in my own strength and wisdom. *It just doesn't work.*

So each time I blow it I have to ask my kids' forgiveness and remind them that I'm still growing to be more like Christ. Then I ask Christ to continue working on me, to make me the best darned dad I can possibly be—one that looks like Him, because He *is* those qualities. He doesn't just point us to them. He *is* them. So when you get Him into your life, you'll have what it takes to become an Immelman Dad.

He'll do the flying for you.

He'll pull you out of the spin. *Any* spin.

More and more I'm meeting guys who admit that their own dads weren't there for them. Many had terrible examples in their home. But when they hear what happens to men like my own father, they realize they, too, can become Immelman Dads.

They can pull out of a flat spin.

They can let go of the stick.

They can experience life on the straight and level once again.

You may have started this book feeling like Walter, chasing a runaway plane. Lots of dads feel that way. Shoot, every veteran dad I know will tell you he still has to review the procedures now and then, because it's easy to forget the basics and fly off out of control. But you can finish this book knowing that one day you'll feel like Mike Mullikin, the seasoned pilot, flying that screaming F-4 off the carrier and into action against the enemy.

With the Holy Spirit as your fuel, you can soar to new heights, win those victories when the bad-dad-attitude attacks come your way, and keep on flying straight and level.

Let go of the stick, turn the controls over to the Father, kick in the afterburner, and let 'er rip!

Just before you put this book down, let me invite you to do what many other dads have done to turn their lives around.

I invite you to ask Jesus Christ to become your pilot.

Let Him turn you into an Immelman Dad. Let Him transform who you are at your very core. Ask Him to pour into your life His wonderful Holy Spirit, the jet fuel and the producer of every wonderful character quality demonstrated in this book. Let Him produce those qualities in your life, starting from the inside out.

If you've never done that, just ask Him. Let go of the stick. He'll be there for you.

Pray something like this: "Lord Jesus, I need You. I admit that I'm a sinner. I confess that, apart from You, I have no hope of heaven. Please come into my life as my Savior and take over as Lord. Forgive me for all of my sins, and by Your Holy Spirit, make me into the man—the husband and father—You want me to be. Amen."

If you have done that and still find yourself slipping into those old habits that leave you exhausted and frustrated, going around in circles, then I invite you to do what I do. Confess that you have been trying to do the Holy Spirit's work for Him, and stop trying to do it on your own strength. Recommit yourself to letting Him work through your life, and submit your will to the Spirit's will.

If you happen to be reading this and you've just now, for the first time in your life, made the decision to trust Christ and have just invited Him into your life, let me say, "Good job, man!" and let me give you a thumbs-up. I didn't know Bob Barden before I met him, but I learned very quickly that I could trust him with my life. In the same way, you might not have known much about Jesus Christ before you started reading this book. But I can tell you from experience, you can trust Him with your life. Start flying with Him as your pilot. Then focus on Him as your landmark.

If you have just let go of the stick for the first time ever, let me also encourage you to talk to someone. Tell someone you know who would be excited about your decision. He or she will help you soar along with other veterans who have learned the art of precision fatherhood flying.

Thanks for letting me pass along a few experiences from my own father, grandfathers, and other mentors in my life. Let me encourage you to seek out mentors of your own—guys who are doin' it right—and let them pass along life's lessons on livin' large by learning how to relate to the little people in your life.

Enjoy your kids and enjoy being the Father's kid. When things go wrong, keep takin' it to the Father. And when things go right, don't forget to give the Father all the credit. Okay?

You've gotten to know quite a bit about me through these stories. I wish I had time to get to know *you*, too. If you know Christ as I do, then I look forward to seeing you some time, in that wonderful place beyond the wild blue yonder the Father is preparing for us after we leave this earth.

We'll have a couple of zillion years to catch up and get to know one another better.

I'll show you some pictures of my kids. They're the greatest.

Happy flying!

See ya.

Final Thanks

———⟨⟨⟨⟩⟩⟩———

At the heart of every book there are silent partners—people God used to write their influence into the author—even if they didn't know it. People like...

Trinity Baptist Church. You faith-family folks patiently endured so many of these stories as sermon illustrations before they were fully mature. Thanks for listening. Thanks for being His family and ours. God is good all the time!

Carolin Pyzik. You have to be the best cheerleader for God's team I've ever met. You just keep taking it to the Father. You're one of the most faithful, ministering members (and church secretaries) I know.

Deb Blohm and Mary Schaap. You and the good people at Sounds of Light Bookstore could have charged me rent for the hours I spent sitting in that rocking chair looking at books on fatherhood. And you could have sent me a bill for baby-sitting for as many times as you kept little Callie company as I was studying or browsing. Sounds of Light is not just a bookstore. It's a ministry.

Dave Blohm. You're the kind of guy every guy needs as a

friend. Through all your personal pain and the grief of losing your dad and sister, God uniquely prepared you to be my shoulder. Courage doesn't mean not feeling. You've shown me the real meaning.

Dave Onisko. You are a true tender warrior and a genuine commando buddy. Your story alone is worth a book. You've handled personal loss with honesty, faith, dignity, and courage. You are an inspiration, pal. How 'bout that cup o' coffee?

Bud and Rae Jean Belt. Are you prophetic or what? Every pastor needs a fellow minister elbowing his ribs to follow God's leading. You two continue to be a matched pair of very positive elbows in our local body.

Jimmie and Tina Avery. How in the world did you know I would need that computer so I could drive Larry crazy at Multnomah with all my e-mail attempts? You dragged me, kicking and screaming, into the electronic age, and I'm forever grateful.

Ron Potter and Joe Fisher. Like stars in the constellation, your Orion experience continues to shed light on good leadership. You are the most encouraging feedback givers I know. You are in the right business for the right reasons, helping leaders lead. I consider it a privilege to be your student.

Jill Potter and Mary Kornacki. Who would have guessed that those critique sessions a decade ago would bear such fruit? Your encouraging words and positive suggestions were bellows, used to fire up my passion for the written word.

Roger Hart. You saw something different and took a chance on printing some opinion page columns that yielded far more than any of us expected. Thanks. You were brought to the job of interim editor "for such a time as this." Congratulations on becoming the "real" editor.

Bob Jodon. It's a privilege to know a newspaper editor who is committed to an even higher standard than mere "objective journalism." You maintain objectivity, yet personally support things that really matter, like marriage and family values. Thanks for giving someone openly associated with Christianity a voice in the secular media.

Ken and Margaret Taylor. Though it was years ago, your hospitality, encouraging words, and your life history of persistence motivated me to try "just once more." The last "once more" was the one that counted.

Bob Riddle. You've shown me the definition of hangin' in. From one shepherd to another, thanks for the encouragement to keep feeding the sheep. You're a pastor's pastor.

Frank Maguire. You have a peculiar way of stirring the creative juices with your portentous word uses. Just when I start feeling like a fobbing, folly-fallen flap-dragon, you and Helen animate our spirits and our vocabulary, helping us to look at life differently—in a good way—and to see ourselves as capable of changing it—in a good way.

Chad DeWeerd and Clayt Carn. My good friends at Friends, and all the fellow carriers of the gonfalon in the Ministerial Association, thanks for including a Baptist boy in your circle. You model for your congregations the fact that there really is only one Jesus. Blessings on you, your families, and all the members of "*The* Church"—all those who serve Christ. Chad said it well: "The higher we lift Him up, and the more in focus He becomes, the smaller and less significant those petty differences appear."

Ron Philips. You taught me how to stop at the hard passages, slow it down until I could correct what's wrong, and do it right, one note at a time, and then work back up to speed. A good lesson on musical passages. A good lesson on life. I'm still working on the transitions. Thanks for teaching much more than music. You are my personal Mr. Holland.

Ed Gore. I really meant it when I asked for honest feedback. Thanks for giving it, and with such encouragement. Your enthusiasm for this project almost matches my own.

Glenn and Leslie Steed. Your basement was a welcome haven when we moved to Michigan. For you to choose to remain our friends after that is amazing! Thanks especially for the gifts of books, including those by James Herriot. Nay, there's nowt funny about t'job of writin', and it's nobbut a great bit of perspiration, but aye, it's as rewardin' as a lambing after complications.

Mike Mullikin. What a unique way for a friendship to take flight! Thanks for becoming the wings beneath my wind and providing the thrust for a chapter that was about to stall.

Stu Weber. You—through your book *Tender Warrior*—were used by God to change my brother-in-law. He told me about the book, so I told our men's group about it, and God has used it to change us all. I wouldn't have been drawn to Multnomah if it hadn't been for your book. Thanks for your leadership through writing.

Kathey Cothern. If you hadn't done so dang well in school ('scuse my French), I wouldn't have had to work so hard to keep up with "the other Cothern kid." Thanks for setting the pace. I love you, Sis. You're the best.

Mom and Dad Castle. You have always been "in our corner." That's amazing, considering that you are in the corner for all seven of your kids. What great role models and what great parents-in-law. Your sacrificial investment in your kids will feed way more than five thousand. I couldn't have chosen better "other" parents if I had tried.

Grandmother Hardcastle. You and Granddaddy taught me to act responsibly, give generously to the Lord's work, and live within our means. Thanks for your lives. They are sermons of the Father's heart at work in the lives of others.

Dad and Mom Cothern. What choice did I have? Dad, you are the most caring pastor, and Mom, you are the most creative writer I know. No wonder it was so hard to figure out what to be when I grew up! You've taught me plenty, but probably the most important concept you taught is that none of us are perfect, just forgiven. Thanks for being willing to admit when you made mistakes. You showed me that there is forgiveness and grace through Jesus Christ. You always insisted that you weren't perfect parents but pointed me to the One who is able to say, "I Am." You did a fine job as parents. Now it's my turn to say, "I'm proud of you." I only hope I can do as well. I promise to "Save the best and forget the rest," and I pray my kids will do the same for me.

Katheryn, Clark III, Callie. Eenie, Meenie, and Minee. You three are probably the strongest three reasons I wrote this book. Thanks for growing up with me. Remember, no matter how many mistakes you and I both make, I still love you and I'll always love you. Keep looking to the Father and keep forgiving people (even your parents) when they blow it. And keep admitting your own mistakes and getting forgiveness from your perfect parent, the Father, because He lives in your hearts and you are in His. He loves you more than I possibly could, and that's a lot!

One final acknowledgment, please.

In nineteen years of marriage I've learned to trust my wife's instincts when it comes to furniture placement. We've moved enough times now that I can recite by memory the typical agenda:

I work up a real lather, straining and grunting, carrying way-heavy boxes to prove my manhood. I, with the help of friends who are too kind to say, "I can't help you move; I'm doing my taxes that day," place the living room furniture where we think Joy would put it.

Joy walks in just as we plop down on a box to watch our muscles twitch. She surveys the room. She puts her hand on her chin. She says, "Hmm." We look at the furniture, then at each other, then at Joy, then back at the furniture, then to our twitching muscles. She smiles. We stand up and ask, "Where do you want it?"

Then she points and we carry, rearranging the room so it looks just the way she wants it. And guess what. The room really *does* look better after she does her pointing routine.

The first twelve times we moved I thought, *Who does she think she is, telling me where to put this furniture?* I just *knew* she would like it the first way. After all, I worked mighty hard on the arrangement. It suited me just fine.

But like most lessons worth learning—the ones that take at least twelve repeats to finally sink in—the lesson on furniture arrangement hit me like a sofa sleeper on the basement stairs, right about the middle of move number thirteen.

I piled the living room furniture in a clump in the middle of the empty space that would become our living room. Then, in a fit of wisdom, I called to my lovely wife, "Honey, where do *you* think we ought to put this stuff?"

Presto chango, she pointed out the finest arrangement of living room furniture a person could want! And the first time, too. Why hadn't I done that the first dozen moves? Because I'm a guy, that's why.

I couldn't admit that Joy actually saw furniture arranging differently than I did. I looked at individual pieces and tried to fit them together where they would fit in certain spaces. She saw the whole arrangement as relationships—this little grouping complementing that little grouping, this table acting as a bridge between these two pieces.

You know, she has a gift. That's what she does. She knows what looks good in the finished product. What "feels" right. The big picture.

Editors are the furniture arrangers of the book world. Those of us who are slow learners like to think our words are divinely inspired the *first* time we put them into the computer. Ha.

After about a dozen rewrites from editors who care enough to give you positive feedback, the lesson on editing sinks in. Rewriting is better writing. And the best writing comes from writers who have great editors. People who have a knack for this sort of thing.

After each of the first twelve article rejects (or book manuscript rejects) you ask, "Who do they think they are, telling me to rearrange these stories? I thought they fit quite nicely the first way."

Then, about midway through manuscript number thirteen, the bell dings, and the light goes on: "Hey, this person knows what he's talking about. He has a knack. This is what he does."

And, sure enough, the really good editors I've worked with suggest "a nice transition here to bridge these two parts more smoothly," "a little color here to complement these two pieces," "a little more detail over here to carry the whole effect to completion," and *poof*, you've got yourself a much better looking finished product.

Not to mention the hundreds of other details they attend to. An editor's job is really a lot more complicated than I was led to believe when I thought they just printed up the divinely inspired words of the writer and people bought it and read it.

I can't help but see the comparison between what editors do and what God does for us as fathers. He shows us the big picture. He helps us learn from our first twelve mistakes. He helps us improve the transitions, arrange the family into a more harmonious grouping, and in general, gives us an overall better finished product.

By this time, my editor is probably either blushing or pulling out the red pencil, getting ready to write, "Delete this part, Cothern. You've gone over the edge."

But really, folks, that's sort of what an editor—and especially the editor of this book, Larry Libby—does. He's got a knack. A gift.

Larry, you're a great furniture arranger when it comes to books. Not only that, but you're in tune with what the Father is doing in the lives of His kids. Thanks.